D!

C000002811

CZECH

D!RTY ®
CZECH

Everyday Slang from
"What's Up?" to "F*%# Off!"

MARTIN BLAHA
illustrated by **LINDSAY MACK**

Ulysses Press

Published by:
Ulysses Press
P.O. Box 3440
Berkeley, CA 94703
www.ulyssespress.com

ISBN: 978-1-56975-871-7
Library of Congress Control Number: 2010937119

Printed in Canada by Transcontinental Printing

10 9 8 7 6 5 4 3 2 1

Acquisitions editor: Kelly Reed
Managing editor: Claire Chun
Editors: Alice Riegert, Katerina Kombercova
Production: Abigail Reser
Proofreader: Lauren Harrison
Interior design: what!design @ whatweb.com
Cover design: Double R Design
Back cover illustration: Lindsay Mack

Distributed by Publishers Group West

For Jaromíra, Hana and Rudolf.
Pro Jaromíra, Hana a Rudolf.

TABLE OF CONTENTS

·····Acknowledgments

Big thanks go to my great friends Alice, Buddy, Motlés and Oscar, to my brother, Petr, and to Charlotta. Love you all.

Thank you Alice, Claire, Kelly and every single person from Ulysses Press who helped make this book happen.

USING THIS BOOK

I wrote this book assuming that you already know enough Czech to get by—to read a menu or order some beers and grub at your local *hospoda* (pub). But whether your knowledge of Czech comes from language podcasts or the college course you almost flunked, slang is usually the last thing you learn after getting down the basics like, "The car is blue," and "Peter is my friend." So if you wanna learn how to pick up girls in Czech or make fun of your friend for being an asshole the night before—keep reading. And even if you don't really know Czech, it couldn't hurt to know how to say, "Let's drink 'til we're fucking wasted."

This book is set up to be as reader friendly as possible. Each phrase is accompanied by its English equivalent. There are example sentences with key slang words bolded so you can break those words out and use them on your own, whether you're just kidding around with your Czech friends at the club or trying to navigate the beautiful streets of Prague, Český Krumlov or some small rural village. And you can be sure that once you start throwing in some slang, even with that thick accent of yours you'll be sure to win some Czech friends. You do have to keep in mind, though, that you can't be using these phrases with any ol' someone. Steer clear of older folks, professionals, government officials, cops and people you just don't know that well. And I hate to say it, but ladies, you better really know the people you're testing these phrases out on, because it isn't really normal for gals to talk like this in the CR.

·····Some basics

You'll be happy to know that boring grammar explanations and conjugation tables are missing from this book (I don't wanna waste your time with stuff you probably already know or don't even care about). On that note, let me just quickly mention a few important grammar-related points and get it out of the way.

TY AND VY

Czech distinguishes between the formal and informal "you." *Ty* (*tykat*) is the informal singular, while *vy* (*vykat*) is the formal singular and plural. *Vy* is also used for the plural informal. Unless they tell you it's okay to use *ty*, always address elders and superiors with the formal *vy*, even if they use the informal *ty* with you. Be aware, though—this book only uses the *ty* form. I mean, if you say some of these phrases to someone you'd speak in the *vy* with (like, say, the customs official), you're gonna come off as a royal ass no matter if you've got the *vy* in there or not.

Here are some distinctions between the formal and informal "you":

Formal (*vy*)	**Informal** (*ty*)
Hello. *Dobrý den*.	Hi. *Ahoj.*
Good evening. *Dobrý večer.*	Bye. *Ahoj or Čau.*
Goodbye. *Nashledanou.*	Take it easy! *Měj se!*

And some possible scenarios:

A hooker to a cop:

> **I had to give you a blow job so I don't get arrested. I think you can use the word *ty* to address me** from now on.
> *Musela jsem Vám ho vykouřit, aby jste mě nezatknul. Myslím, že od ted'ka mi můžete tykat.*

A neighbor to a neighbor:

> **Mrs. Dana, we've slept together three times already; shall we use *ty* now?**
> *Paní Dano, už jsme spolu třikrát spali, můžem si už tykat?*

During intercourse:

> **It's already in. We can use the word *ty* now.**
> *Už je tam. Můžem si už tykat.*

CASES

The Czech language has seven grammatical cases (or declensions) of nouns, pronouns and adjectives. WTF? It just means that the endings of words change depending on their function in the sentence (direct object, indirect object, location, etc.) — it's like conjugating a verb but with nouns, pronouns and adjectives. When words are listed alone in this book, they're in the nominative case. However, when they're given in phrases, they have whatever case ending is necessary for the grammatical context.

GENDER

Czech nouns are masculine, feminine or neuter. Masculine words end in consonants, as in *pán* (mister), *muž* (man) and *bratr* (brother). Feminine words mostly end in the vowels "a" and "e," as in *žena* (woman) and *růže* (rose), or a soft consonant "ň," as in *píseň* (song). Neuter words end in the vowels "o," as in *křeslo* (chair), and "e" or "ě," as in *dítě* (child).

For people, both adjectives and the past tenses of verbs take different endings depending on whether you're talking about a man or a woman. This book uses the masculine form as the default, or lists it first when there's a male/female distinction.

In formal Czech, adjectives following masculine words end in the vowel "ý," as in *ten pán je mladý* (the man is young). Adjectives corresponding to feminine words end in the vowel "á," as in *ta růže je krásná* (the rose is beautiful). Neuter adjectives end in vowel "é," as in to *dítě je malé* (the child is small). Because this is a slang book, it mostly uses the slang ending for masculine adjectives, "ej," as in *ten pán je mladej* (the man is young), and the slang ending for neuter adjectives "ý," as in *to dítě je malý* (the child is small); both are commonly used in Prague and Bohemia. The feminine adjective ending is always "á" in both formal and informal speech.

PRONUNCIATION

Czech is a very phonetic language (one letter equals one sound), so when you know how to spell a word, you know how to pronounce it, too. Oh, and all Czech words are stressed on the first syllable.

·····Pronouncing Czech

The Czech alphabet has 40 letters—the diacritic marks not only mean you pronounce the letters differently, they also make them completely separate letters. The letter "ř" is unique to the Czech language, and its pronunciation is so difficult that many children of Czech speakers have to be specially taught how to say it. If you want to try to achieve the sound, it's pronounced sort of like an "r" with "zh," as in Dvořák (*dvoržhák*). But if you pronounce it as an "r," people will understand you.

Here's the Czech alphabet:

a sounds like "u" in fun.

á sounds like "a" in father.

b sounds like "b" in bank, but at the end of a word it sounds like "p" in "shop."

c sounds like the "ts" in bits.

č sounds like the "ch" in church.

d sounds like "d" in dog.

ď sounds like the "du" in due or duty in British English.

dž sounds like "dj," as in gin and juice. It's not a letter of the alphabet, but it's used a lot.

e sounds like "eh," as in excellent.

é sounds like a prolonged "a" like in care

ě sounds like "ye" in yes.

f sounds like "f" in frog.

g sounds like "g" in leg.

h sounds like "h" in hot.

ch sounds like "k" in cock.

i sounds like a short "i" as in ship.

í sounds like a prolonged "ee," as in sheep.

j sounds like "y" in yellow.

k sounds like "k" in kitchen.

l sounds like "l" in lion.

m sounds like "m" in mat.

n sounds like "n" in nut.

ň sounds like a soft "ni," as in onion.

o sounds like "o," as in lost.

ó sounds like a prolonged "o" in or.

p sounds like "p" in plum.

q sounds like "kw," as in quilt.

r sounds like "r" in the Spanish word *gringo*; it's trilled.

ř sounds like "rzh," a rolled "r" followed immediately by "zh."

s sounds like "s" in summer.

š sounds like the "sh" in shower.

t sounds like "t" in Tom.

ť sounds like a soft "tu," as in Tuesday.

u sounds like "u" in push.

ů, **ú** sound like a prolonged "oo," as in tooth.

v sounds like "v" in victory.

w also sounds like "v" in victory.

x sounds like "ks," as in tax.

y sounds like a short "y," as in Lynn.

ý sounds like prolonged the "ee" in deep.

z sounds like "z" in zebra, but at the end of a word it sounds like "s."

ž sounds like "zh" as in pleasure.

Some Czech words don't have any vowels at all, like *strč prst skrz krk* ("stick a finger through your throat"). Okay, you might not be using this one very often, but there's other cool stuff in this book you'll use over and over again. So keep your finger out of your throat, take your *Dirty Czech* and get dirty with it!

CHAPTER 1

HOWDY CZECH

NAZDÁREK ČEŠTINA

Your first impression of Czechs may be that they're cold and standoffish toward people they've just met, at least compared to overly familiar Americans. Maybe it's because they live in a cold climate where they don't see much sun for nearly half the year. But more likely it's because they're more formal and tend to be more polite when meeting new peeps than, let's say, excessively friendly Americans. Once they get to know you though, you'll find that Czechs are warm, engaging and affable.

·····Hello!
Dobrý den!

Dobrý den paired with a firm handshake is used when you're meeting someone for the first time, hooking up with your friends, asking a stranger for information or any number of generic encounters you have during the course of the day. After sunset, though, you'll want to use *dobrý večer* (good evening) to avoid the risk of being spotted as a dorky tourist.

Hello, what time is it?
Dobrý den, kolik je hodin, prosím?

Hi
Ahoj

Hi everyone!
Ahoj všichni!

Hey
Čau

Holla
Čus

Cheers!
Zdravíčko!
Literally, "little health." You can use this one to wish someone a good day, but it's not used when toasting.

Yo!
Hej!

Hiya!
Čauky!

Good afternoon
Dobré odpoledne

Good evening
Dobrý večer

Good night
Dobrou noc

Wassup dudes!
Nazdar frajeři!

Whaddup!
Zduř!

Howdy, sexy ladies.
Nazdárek, kočky.
Kočky literally means "cats."

Good morning, where are my boxers?
Dobré ráno, kde mám trenky?

Greetings!
Zdravím!

What's up, dogg?
Co je, vole?
Literally, "What's up, ox?" You can use this as an insult or to address a good friend. The difference is in the tone.

How ya doin'?
Jak to de?

What's new?
Co je novýho?

What's happening?
Co se děje?

What's good?
Jak se daří?

How's life?
Jak jde život?

·····How are you?
Jak se máš?

Americans usually follow up "Hello" with a compulsive "How are you?" or "How's it going?" Czech speakers, on the other hand, don't use these questions as rote responses unless they genuinely want to know how you are, making the phrases immensely more meaningful.

Hi Dan, how's it going today?
Ahoj Dane, jak se dnes vede?

I'm pretty hungover.
Mám pěknou kocovinu.

I'm great!
Mám se skvěle!

Excellent!
Výborně!

INTRODUCE YOURSELF)))
PŘEDSTAV SE!

My name is Dana and I'm from Eastwick.
Jmenuji se Dana a jsem z Eastwicku.

I'm 19 years old, I like to drink beer and I just shaved my beaver.
Je mi 19 let, ráda piju pivo a právě jsem si oholila bobra.

Hi, I'm Karel.
Ahoj, já jsem Karel.

I live in Brno and I'm hung like a donkey.
Žiju v Brně a mám velkou kládu.

Fine.
Fajn.

Super!
Supr!

It's going all right.
Jde to.

Same old, same old.
Všechno při starým.

And you?
A ty?

Chillin'!
Pohoda!

Chilaxin!
Pohodička!

So, so. It could be better.
Nic moc. Mohlo by to být lepší.

It sucks!
Stojí to za hovno!
Literally, "It shits."

It's terrible, my bf / gf just dumped me.
*Je to hrozný, **můj starej / moje stará** mi zrovna dal / dala kopačky.*
Literally, "my old one." You can use this when you talk about your boyfriend or girlfriend if they're annoying you or if you're just messing around.

Don't even ask, my bf just kicked me out of the apartment.
Ani se neptej, můj starej mě zrovna vykopl z bytu.

Bummer, but you can sleep at my place.
To je na prd, můžeš ale spát u mě.

Horrible.
Strašný.

Shitty.
Na hovno.

It totally sucks.
Je to fakt v prdeli.

I don't even wanna talk about it.
Ani o tom nechci mluvit.

·····Nice to meet you!
Těší mě!

A great way to start chatting with your Czechs and find out more about them is to let them know a little bit about yourself. They may seem too curious or nosey, but keep in mind that their interest in you is always a good sign.

Nice to meet you...
Těší mě...

Mr. Novák.
pane Novák.

Ms. Nováková.
paní Nováková.
Czech female surnames very often end with *-á* or *-ová*. You can also see this in magazines and newspapers when they mention American females, like Paris Hiltonová.

young lady.
mladá paní.

young man.
mladý pane.

buddy.
kámo.

I'm glad to finally meet you.
Jsem rád / ráda, že tě konečně poznávám.

The pleasure is mine.
Potěšení je na mé straně.

Ladies and gentlemen! It's my honor to introduce you to…
Dámy a pánové! Je mi ctí vám představit…

   my co-worker.
   mého kolegu / mojí kolegyni.

   my classmate.
   mého spolužáka / mojí spolužačku.

   the biggest asshole in the world.
   největšího hajzla na světě.

I have the day off and I'm bored.
Mám dnes volno a nudím se.

Do you wanna go out tonight?
Chceš dnes večer někam vyrazit?

Sure! Where?
Jasně! Kam?

Where are you from?
Odkud jsi?

Do you like your job?
Líbí se ti tvá práce?

Here's my business card.
Tady je moje vizitka.

Can I have your phone number?
Můžeš mi dát tvoje číslo?

How long have you lived here?
Jak dlouho tady žiješ?

Can I show you around?
Můžu ti to tady ukázat?

Can you show me the city?
Můžeš mi ukázat město?

Where should we meet?
Kde se sejdeme?

I'll leave it up to you.
Nechám to na tobě.

I like it here a lot.
Moc se mi tu líbí.

·····Long time no see!
Dlouho jsme se neviděli!

It's always nice to randomly bump into your old buddies on the street. But doesn't it suck when you run into people you don't wanna talk to and you end up having to catch up with them and blah blah blah? Here are some polite phrases to use when it's too late to pretend you didn't see 'em.

It's nice to see you again.
Jsem rád / ráda, že tě zas vidím.

I'm glad you stopped by.
Jsem rád / ráda, že ses stavil / stavila.

Finally! I almost thought I'd never see you again!
Konečně! Už jsem myslel, že tě nikdy neuvidím!

What the heck are you doing here?
Co tady sakra děláš?

I've been thinking about you.
Myslel / Myslela jsem na tebe.

I don't believe it! Is it you?
To není možný! Jsi to ty?

You look great!
Vypadáš skvěle!

You look like shit!
Vypadáš hrozně!

Do you have time to grab a beer?
Máš čas si dát pivo?

·····Please and thank you
Prosím a děkuji

If there's one word to learn in Czech, it's *prosím*. It means "please," "you're welcome" and "excuse me!?" It can even be used as "hello" when answering the phone: *Ano, prosím?* (Yes, please?). So when you get a brain fart and don't know what to say, at least be polite and say "please."

Please.
Prosím.

Pretty please!
Pěkně prosím!

Help me out!
Pomož mi!

I'm begging you!
Já tě prosím.

Don't be a pussy, and try it, pleaz!
Nebuď posera a zkus to, prosim tě!

Can you do me a favor?
Můžu tě požádat o laskavost?

What's that? I didn't hear you.
Co to? Neslyšel / Neslyšela jsem tě.

'Scuse me, comin' through!
S dovolením!

Well, excuuuse me!
Pardón!

Finally!
No konečně!

Are you fucking kidding me!?
Ty si snad děláš srandu!?

Thank you!
Děkuji!

Thanks!
Dík!

Thanks a lot!
Díky moc!

> **You just spilled red wine all over my bra,
> thanks a lot!**
> *Teď jsi mi polil / polila podprdu sklenicí červenýho,
> díky moc!*

Thanks for trying, buddy!
Díky za snahu, kámo!

Sure. No problem!
Jistě. To to není problém!

You're welcome!
Není zač!

·····Sorry!
Promiň!

If you're a natural klutz or just a true fuckup, then you're
already familiar with these English terms.

> **Sorry for being late.**
> ***Promiň**, že jdu pozdě.*

> **I apologize for stepping on your foot.**
> ***Omlouvám se**, že jsem ti šlápnul / šlápla na nohu.*

> **I'm really sorry about that.**
> *To mě opravdu mrzí.*

Oops!
Jejda!

My bad!
Sory!

It's my fault.
To je moje chyba.

Just kidding!
Dělám si srandu!

Pardon me?
Co prosím?

It's not a big deal.
Nic se neděje.

No biggy!
To nic!

It's OK.
To je v pořádku.

No problem.
To není problém.

Don't worry about it!
Z toho si nic nedělej!

·····Goodbye
Na shledanou

Goodbye
Na shledanou
Literally, "until we see each other."

Bye
Ahoj
When you say "hello," I say "goodbye." In Czech, we're saying the same thing: *ahoj* or *čau*, which are used for both greetings. If you're saying an informal "bye" to an elderly person, teacher, etc., use *nashle* (an informal abbreviation of *nashledanou*).

Thank you for a nice evening!
Děkuji za pěkný večer!

See ya later!
Tak zatím!

Later.
Uvidíme se.

Have a safe trip.
Šťastnou cestu.

Bye y'all.
Mějte se.

Take care!
Měj se!

Later!
Zatím!

Call me!
Zavolej mi!

Give me a ring!
Brnkni mi!

Text me!
Textni mi!

I gotta go.
Musím jít.

I'm outta here.
Jdu pryč.

I'm bouncing.
Já mizím.

I have to leave.
Musím odejít.

I'm out.
Jdu pryč.

See you soon.
Tak zatím.

I'm off.
Já padám.

Let's get outta here!
Mizíme!

CHAPTER 2

FRIENDLY CZECH
PŘÁTELSKÁ ČEŠTINA

•••••Friends
Kamarádi

Unlike Americans, Czechs don't call everyone they know or just met a friend. And just because a Czech starts to use the informal *ty* with you, it sure as hell doesn't mean you're BFFs. But don't get me wrong—Czechs are cordial and awesome pals because when they do consider you a true friend, it means they're in it for the long haul. So you're probably not going to be called *kamarád/kamarádka* when you meet a Czech for the first time, but that doesn't mean you can't strike up some polite small talk. Czechs are often curious about foreign cultures and customs, so talking about your own traditions and experiences can't hurt.

Buddy
Kámoš / Kámoška

Honza may be my **buddy,** but sometimes I just wanna kick his ass.
*Honza je sice můj **kámoš**, ale někdy bych mu nakopal prdel.*

Adéla is a **chill girl,** but sometimes gets on my nerves cuz she gabs all the time.
*Adéla je **pohodová holka**, ale někdy mi leze na nervy, protože furt kecá.*

Those are my **girls.**
*To jsou moje **holky**.*

He's my **boy.**
*Je to můj **kluk**.*

What up, **homie**?
*Jak to jde, **parťáku**?*

How are you, **dogg**?
*Jak se máš, **vole**?*

Hey **bro**!
*Hej **kámo**!*

They're **best friends.**
*Jsou to **nejlepší kamarádi / kamarádky**.*

She really needs a **gossip buddy.**
*Ona fakt potřebuje **kámoše / kámošku na drby**.*

Boyfriend / Girlfriend
Přítel / Přítelkyně

> So that wimp is her **boyfriend**?
> *Tak tenhle jouda je její **přítel**?*

> What a fine ass...oh, she's your **girlfriend**?
> *To je ale kus...jé, to je tvoje **přítelkyně**?*

Fiancé / Fiancée
Snoubenec / Snoubenka

> Romana met her **fiancé** on the Internet.
> *Romana se seznámila se svým **snoubencem** na internetu.*

Booty call
Kluk do postele / Holka do postele

Fuck Buddy
Nabíječ / Šukna

> **She's not only his boss, but also his fuck buddy.**
> *Ona není jenom jeho šéfová, ale i jeho šukna.*
> This is pretty rude, so you might not want to actually say it in front of that special someone.

He's / She's my...
On / Ona je můj / moje...

> **partner.**
> *partner / partnerka.*

> **lover.**
> *milenec / milenka.*

> **ex.**
> *bejvalej / bejvalá.*
> You can also just use the English word "ex."

> **hubby.**
> *manžílek.*

> **wifey.**
> *ženuška.*

·····Hey dogg!
Hele vole!

Czechs don't usually curse in public, but the rules are different among close friends and acquaintances.

Just like Americans call their good friends "man," "dude" or "dogg," Czechs affectionately use *vůl* ("ox") when addressing each other or as a filler. If you don't want to piss off your Czech friend, only use *Ty vole!* ("You ox!") when you both know each other well and when you're just shooting the shit. If you call a stranger or old man *Vole!*, you're looking to start a fight, but talking to your homies, you can call them pretty much anything.

> **Hi man, what's up?**
> *Ahoj chlape, jak to jde?*

Hey dogg, look at those tits!
Hele vole, koukej na ty kozy!

Dudes, let's play soccer after work.
Frajeři, pojďte si po práci zahrát fotbal.

C'mon dogg, don't be a pussy!
Dělej vole, nebuď posera!

What's the news?
Co je novýho?

·····Great!

Skvělý!

Tired of using the tried-and-true "cool" to express yourself?
Here are a few more ways to show your excitement:

It's…
To je…

> **cool.**
> *paráda.*

> **excellent.**
> *výborný.*

> **perfect.**
> *perfektní.*

> **super.**
> *supr.*

> **neat.**
> *príma.*

> **the best.**
> *nejlepší.*

> **da bomb!**
> *bomba!*

> **a surprise.**
> *překvapení.*

That's rad.
To nemá chybu.
Literally, "It has no flaw."

It's not a bad idea.
To není špatnej nápad.

Awesome!
Boží!
Literally, "It's godlike!"

Sure thing, let's do it.
Jasná zpráva, jdem do toho.

Now you're talking.
To si dám líbit!

TERMS OF ENDEARMENT)))
SLOVÍČKA LÁSKY

Dear
Drahý / Drahá

You're my...
Jsi můj / moje...

sweetie.
drahoušek.

sunshine.
sluníčko.

love.
láska.

little cutie.
kocourek / kočička.
Literally, "my little cat."

honey.
zlatíčko.

angel.
andílek.

darling.
miláček.

cutey.
buclík / boubelka.
Literally, "chubster." Don't worry, this is used for our loved ones who have a few extra kilos here and there.

dumpling.
budulínek.

pumpkin.
melounek.
Literally, "little melon."

sugar.
cukrouš.

You're my **number one**!
*Ty jsi moje **jednička**!*

Ain't you just the **sweetest thing**!
*Ty jsi ale **zlatíčko**!*
Literally, "little gold."

·····Time for a little romance
Čas na romantiku

Trying to score some Czech chicks? Then don't be shy about telling a girl how great she is. After all your sweet talkin', ask her on a date. FYI: Guys generally make the first move and are expected to work for the payoff. When taking your date out, you gotta show her some gentlemanly manners—open doors, pull out the chair in a restaurant, offer a hand when getting in or out of a car, etc. But don't follow the "lady first" rule when entering a pub. A man should always go in before his date to protect his lady friend from getting hit on. Oh, and if you decide to bring your date flowers, make sure you give her an odd number of blooms; it's bad luck to give an even amount.

Where can I pick up some chicks around here?
Kde tady můžu sbalit nějaký baby?

How old are you?
Kolik ti je let?

Are you single?
Chodíš s někým?

Do you live alone?
Bydlíš sám / sama?

Are you free tonight?
Máš dnes večer čas?

Jůlie is so hot, all the men hit on her.
Jůlie je fakt kost, všichni chlapi za ní lezou.

You are a really cool girl.
Jsi moc parádní holka.

That guy is super lame.
Ten kluk je úplně mimo.

Can I get your number?
Můžeš mi dát tvoje číslo?

Vanessa finally went on a date last night.
Vanessa šla včera večer konečně na rande.

I'm totally digging you.
Totálně tě žeru.

I like you.
Líbíš se mi.
Líbíš se mi is a more superficial way of saying you dig someone.

I care about you.
Mám tě rád. / Mám tě ráda.
This phrase may get you some, but it's kind of an asshole thing to say since in Czech you only use this line if you genuinely like the person and are serious about him or her.

I love you!
Miluju tě!
Again, only used for people you actually love.

Do you wanna go to my place?
Chceš jít ke mě domů?

She's totally your type, bro!
Ta je přesně tvůj typ, kámo!

·····Mom and dad and the whole damn fam
Máma a táta a celá rodina

Like everyone else in the world, Czechs either love or hate their families, and some just ignore them, but for most, family is where it's at.

Mother
Matka

Mom
Máma

Mommy
Mamča

Father
Otec

> **My father is a huge soccer fan.**
> *Můj otec je hroznej fotbalovej fanda.*

Dad
Táta

Daddy
Taťka

Sister
Sestra

Sis
Ségra

> **Karolina's like my sis—we can gab over nothing all day long.**
> *Karolína je jak moje ségra—můžem kecat o ničem celý den.*

Brother
Brácha

Uncle
Strejda

Aunt
Teta

> **My aunt can feed the whole army with her dumplings.**
> *Moje teta vždycky navaří knedlíků jak pro celou armádu.*

Grandma
Babička

Grandpa
Děda

Her old man has always made her life miserable.
Její fotr jí vždy dělal ze života peklo.

Stepfather
Nevlastní otec ; Otčím

Stepmother
Nevlastní matka ; Macecha
Macecha is used in the evil stepmother kind of way.

•••••Acquaintances, colleagues and enemies
Známí, kolegové a nepřátelé

Have you ever had any acquaintances or coworkers who became your enemies? Or enemies who became your friends or even fuck buddies? Here's a way to distinguish between 'em.

Acquaintance
Známý / Známá

She's just **someone I know** from dancing lessons.
Je to jen jedna známá z tanečních.

I'm telling you, don't talk to **strangers** or you'll get ass-raped one day!
Říkám ti, nebav se s cizíma lidma, nebo tě jednou někdo znásilní!

All my **coworkers** are super chill.
Všichni moji spolupracovníci jsou naprostý pohodáři.

We are a great **team**.
Jsme skvělý tým.

Boss
Šéf / Šéfová

No wonder he became a **manager** so fast—he's such a kiss-ass.
Nedivím se, že se stal manažerem tak rychle—je to vlezdoprdelka.

Vlasta's **supervisor** hates her and always talks shit about her.
Vlastin vedoucí ji nesnáší a pořád jí pomlouvá.

Watch out, everybody knows he's a back-stabber.
Dávej si bacha, každej ví, že je to podrazák.

Don't be an ass!
Nepruď!

We don't get along at all.
Vůbec spolu nevycházíme.

He / She gets on my nerves.
Leze mi na nervy.

We don't like each other.
Nemáme se rádi.

That fool is my enemy.
Ten blbec je můj nepřítel.

Arch nemesis
Úhlavní nepřítel

·····Personalities and characters
Osobnosti a charaktery

As the Czech saying goes, "There's a few different types of people in the world. Some of them are dumb and all the others are stupid." But even the stupid ones have other attributes…

He / She is so…
On / Ona je tak…

> **stupid.**
> *stupidní.*
>
> **dumb.**
> *hloupej / hloupá.*
>
> **ridiculous.**
> *nemožnej / nemožná.*
>
> **annoying.**
> *otravnej / otravná.*
>
> **stubborn.**
> *tvrdohlavej / tvrdohlavá.*

mean.
zlej / zlá.

vulgar.
sprostej / sprostá.

cold-hearted.
bezcitnej / bezcitná.

full of drama.
hysterka.

Nerd
Šprt / Šprtka

Mary isn't actually smart, she's just a nerd.
Mary není zas tak chytrá, je to jen šprtka.

He thinks he knows everything, smart-ass.
Myslí si, že ví všechno nejlíp, chytrák.

Geez, you are so gosh darn…
Ježiš ty jseš fakt tak…

smart.
chytrej / chytrá.

likeable.
sympatickej / sympatická.

nice.
hodnej / hodná.

chill.
pohodovej / pohodová.

She's the perfect chick, I totally dig her.
Ona je perfektní buchta, totálně ji žeru.

All the guys are crazy about her.
Všichni kluci po ní šílí.

You're the shit, man.
Ty seš držák, chlape.

Lumír is a no-bullshit kinda guy.
Lumír je přímovej kluk.

She doesn't mess around.
Ta se s tím nesere.

She's only into jocks—you've got no chance.
Ta je jen na rampy—nemáš u ní šanci.

Damn! That broad is a fox!
Ty jo! Ta ženská je kost!

Even though he's married, he's still a man-whore.
I když je ženatej, je to pořád děvkař.

I don't know what to think of her, she's such a fake.
Nevím, co si mám o ní myslet, pořád se přetvařuje.

What a(n)…
To je ale…

> **idiot.**
> *idiot.*

> **moron.**
> *debil / debilka.*

> **fuckup.**
> *zmrd.*

> **nutcase.**
> *cvok.*

> **psycho.**
> *šílenec / šílenkyně.*

Everybody knows she's crazy.
Každej ví, že je blázen.

Don't even think about dating him, he's a…
Ani na to nemysli s ním chodit, je to…

He / She is such a…
On / Ona je takovej / taková…

> **slacker.**
> *flákač / flákačka.*

> **weirdo.**
> *podivín / podivínka.*

> **snob.**
> *snob / snobka.*

He's / She's clueless.
Neví, která bije.

He's / She's lazy as a pig.
Je línej / líná jako prase.

That lazy ass just slacks off all day.
Ten lenoch se celý den jen fláká.

Blabbermouth
Slepičí prdel
Literally, "hen's ass."

Don't tell her anything, she's a blabbermouth.
Nic jí neříkej, je to slepičí prdel.

Karolína's got a big mouth.
Karolína všechno vykecá.

·····Just your everyday…
Je to normální…

Mama's boy
Mámin mazel

Daddy's girl
Tátův mazlík

Gossip
Drbna

> **My neighbor is the biggest gossip.**
> *Můj soused je největší drbna.*

Flake
Křivák

Old geezer
Staroch

Dork
Trdlo

Pimp
Pasák

Slut
Štětka

Sleeze
Hnusák

Bighead
Náfuka

Retard
Magor

Jerk
Blbec

Punk
Pankáč

Hippie
Hipízák / Hipízačka

Rocker
Roker / Rokerka

Poser
Pozér / Pozérka

Wannabe
Nicka

Whore
Kurva

Loser
Ztracená existence

Pretty boy
Hezoun

Spoiled brat
Rozmazlenec

Bitch
Čubka ; Mrcha

Ho
Šlapka

Player
Hráč

CHAPTER 3

PARTY CZECH
PAŘÍCÍ ČEŠTINA

Czechs always seem to find an excuse to go out socializing and drinking—it's your birthday, work's over, the sun is out, tomorrow is another day…hell, who needs an excuse to get toasted? *Jdeme pařit* (Let's party)!

•••••It's party time!
Jde se pařit!

If you party with Czechs, you will drink. A lot. Maybe more (or maybe less, you boozer) than what you're used to back home. But you probably won't be sipping martinis and Manhattans or throwing back premium tequila shots. When Czechs choose their poison, it's in the form of local beer and wine, and Becherovka (sweet herbal liqueur) or Fernet (very dark and bitter herbal liqueur) shots. And while Gatorade may be a standard hangover cure in the States, garlic-bouillon soup or another glass of beer is where it's at in the Czech Republic.

> **It's my birthday today—let's get trashed.**
> *Dneska mám narozeniny—dem se ožrat.*

> **Congratulations!**
> *Blahopřeju!*

Congrats on the new hair plugs—it looks so natural.
Gratuluju, ty nastřelený vlasy vypadají jak pravý.

Where's the **party** at?
*Kde se dnes **paří**?*
You can also use the word "party" and everyone'll know what you're talking about.

Were you invited to Anna's bash?
Jseš pozvanej / pozvaná na Annin večírek?

You can't miss it. It'll be fun.
To si nesmíš nechat ujít. Bude to sranda.

We gotta **celebrate**!
*To se musí **oslavit**!*

Come to the party. Maybe you'll finally get some action.
Pojď na tu pařbu. Možná si už konečně vrzneš.

He's getting hitched soon, let's find him a good blowey.
Za chvíli jde do chomoutu, pojď mu najít nějakou holku, co mu ho dobře vykouří.

I wanna…
Chci…

> go downtown.
> *jít do města. ; jít do centra.*

> go to the club.
> *jít na diskotéku.*

> get my groove on.
> *si povyrazit.*

> celebrate all night long.
> *slavit celou noc.*

party hard core tonight.
dnes pořádně zapařit.

go to that party your bro was talking about.
jít na tu pařbu, o které mluvil tvůj kámoš.

Let's go…
Pojďme…

get our drink on!
popít!

drink to it!
to zapít!

get smashed.
se zbořit.

get hammered.
se zmastit.

out for a drink.
si dát něco k pití.

take shots.
na panáka.

drink some wine.
na víno.

·····What's the plan?
Co máme v plánu?

No one likes to party alone. And if you do, that's pretty sad. So if you feel like having some good old-fashioned fun with your homies, try some of these phrases out.

What are we gonna do today?
Co dneska podnikem?

Do you wanna party hard with me tonight?
Chceš dnes večer se mnou dobře zapařit?

Whatta ya up for this weekend?
Máš nějaké plány na víkend?

Let's find us some sexy broads tonight.
Pojď dnes večer sbalit nějaký sexy ženský.

I can't, bro. I found myself a great chick earlier today.
Nemůžu, kámo. Dnes ráno jsem sbalil skvělou buchtu.

I'm **bored** out of my skull.
Nudím *se k smrti.*

I'm **gonna have fun** tonight.
Dnes večer **si to užiju**.

Dunno, what do you think?
Nevim, co myslíš?

Something fun.
Nějakou srandu.

Bring it on!
Rozjeď to!

I'm about to **get freaky** on the dance floor.
Pořádně to na parketu **rozjedu**.

Ester's **going pretty wild!**
Ester **se pěkně rozdivočila!**

She knows how to **rage**.
Umí to **pořádně rozbalit**.

HAPPY NAME DAY!)))
VŠE NEJLEPŠÍ K SVÁTKU!

Name day? Based on the Catholic calendar of saints, the Czech calendar has a name associated with pretty much every day of the year. It includes your average Joe saints, like Peter (Petr) or John (Jan), and some Czech saints, like Anežka, Wenceslas and Václav. But over time, other popular names were added since everyone wants to celebrate their name day, right? And let's face it, with a country where almost half the population claims to be atheist, there's no religious pressure to name your kid after a saint. If your name's not on the calendar, just find some rendition of it and proclaim it your name day. I mean, it's really just become a good excuse to celebrate with some booze or to get chocolates and presents.

Lukáš doesn't know when to stop.
Lukáš nikdy neví, kdy přestat.

I'm having a blast!
Perfektně se bavím!

I'm fucking enjoying this!
Užívám si to na plný koule!

Are ya up for…
Chceš…

> **pubhopping?**
> *vyrazit po hospodách?*

> **barhopping?**
> *vyrazit do barů?*

Hey, let's go…
Hele, pojď…

> **to that neighborhood joint you were talking about.**
> *do té místní knajpy, kterou jsi zmiňoval / zmiňovala.*

> **to the brothel.**
> *do bordelu.*

> **to the strip club to check out some titties.**
> *na striptýz vomrknout nějaký ty kozičky.*

> **home now.**
> *už domů.*

This club is really bumpin'.
Tenhle klub fakt žije.

·····Relaxing
Relaxace

Even hard-core partiers need a break every once in a while.

> **I'm gonna rest for a while.**
> *Na chvíli si odpočinu.*

> **Chill for a bit!**
> *Dej si na chvíli voraz!*

I'm just **gonna take it easy** tonight and stay at home.
*Dnes večer **si dám klídek** a zůstanu doma.*

My ass has been glued to the couch all day. Let's **stay in** and watch TV.
*Celej den si válím prdel na gauči. Pojď **zůstat doma** a koukat na televizi.*

I'm not going anywhere tonight.
Dnes večer nikam nejdu.

I'm...
Jsem...

> tired.
> *utahanej / utahaná.*

> pooped.
> *hotovej / hotová.*

> really lazy.
> *fakt línej / líná.*
> If you really want to ramp up the lazy, say *Dneska jsem línej jako prase*, which translates as "I'm as lazy as a pig today."

> so fried.
> *úplně mrtvej.*
> Literally, "completely dead."

> sleepy.
> *ospalej.*

I'm beat. I need a little snooze.
Jsem vyřízenej. Potřebuju si schrupnout.

Let's **take a nap.**
*Pojďme si **dát šlofíka**.*

·····Where Czechs like to drink
Kde Češi rádi popíjejí

It's easy to get booze in the Czech Republic; pubs, clubs and wine bars are everywhere. Pub life is so big in the CR that they even have a saying, *Bez peněz do hospody nelez*

(Never go to the pub without money)…cuz you know you're gonna be there a while, and those rounds that keep coming sure aren't free.

Pub
Hospoda

A pub is the best place to get your drink on. You can get a variety of beers fresh on tap, lots of cheap shots, plus traditional Czech dishes. But the quality of food varies a lot, so if you care about the grub, ask around for the locals' favorites.

Beerhouse
Pivnice

Looking for cheap booze? Then a *pivnice* is where you should park your butt. It's dirty, noisy, thick with smoke and full of happy, drunk Czechs. It really is all about the alcohol here; food is pretty limited—sometimes all they've got is potato chips and warm sausages. Nowadays, some beerhouses and breweries (*pivovary*) offer a full menu of tasty dishes, so take your pick depending on what you're in the mood for.

Inn
Hostinec

Just a tiny step up from a *pivnice*, a *hostinec* has more booze plus more food choices of slightly better quality. And if you're lucky, the service might be pretty good, too.

Wine bar
Vinárna

Another cool spot to get some drinks, a *vinárna* is lot cleaner and more subdued than a pub. Wine is often served right out of the barrel, but you can also order by the bottle. They may serve cocktails, hard alcohol and dinner, too.

Wine cellar
Vinný sklípek

Wine is the true highlight at a *vinný sklípek*, where you'll find light snacks (like cheese or a salami plate) to complement the vintages, but not much else in the way of food.

Café
Kavárna
Part café, part bar, *kavárny* are all over Prague and other cities.
Here you can read the newspaper, get a Viennese coffee
(*Vídeňská káva*; topped with a big scoop of whipped cream) or
Algerian coffee (*Alžírská káva;* served with whipped cream and
egg liqueur), beer, liquor and a variety of desserts and snacks.
With the old-time atmosphere and Gothic architecture, you'll feel
like you were transported back to the 1920s.

Dance club
Diskotéka ; Díza
Czechs love to listen to music and dance while getting
hammered, hanging out with friends or looking for a one-night
stand. If you don't feel like dancing, you can just sit at the bar in
the *díza* and peoplewatch.

Nightclub
Noční klub
You can catch many internationally known DJs mixing on the
turntables in Prague's biggest nightclubs.

Jazz club / Rock bar
Jazzový klub / Rockový bar
These are smaller venues where you can see bands and rock out
to some heavy metal or groove to some jazz, rock or bluegrass
while slurping down some booze.

Lounge
Bar
The Czech word *bar* is best translated to what Americans think
of as a lounge—a modern, chic place where you can get drunk
while sipping overpriced cocktails in the company of all the trendy,
good-looking, "cool" and successful (or unsuccessful) hipsters.

Dive bar
Nonstop
Nonstopy are the Czech answer to dirty American dive bars with
cheap drinks and rude, crappy service. You usually end up in a
nonstop at 5 a.m. when everything else is closed. You can dance
your drunken ass off or play *automaty* (slot machines) all you
want and nobody cares (or remembers). And yes, they are open
nonstop.

Concert arena
Koncertní hala

These are the same as in any big city all over the world. You can catch many popular bands and singers performing during their European tours in Prague, Brno or Ostrava. The Czech audience is mostly wilder and louder than American fans. Czechs rarely sit during the performance, and they like to dance, jump, shout and go nuts.

·····Flying the rainbow flag
Let na duhové vlajce

Yup, that's right, the Czech Republic is one of the most gay-friendly countries. In fact, gay couples get nearly the same benefits that straight couples do, so the CR has become a popular destination for the LGBT community. It's got everything from fetish clubs (*fetiš kluby*) to erotic shows (*erotické show*) to your average cabaret and drag shows. Don't forget that Czechs are friendly, they like meeting new people and they make for good eye candy.

Are there any gay bars around?
Jsou tady někde gay bary?

This is the best drag show in town.
To je nejlepší travesti show ve městě.

Gay club
Gay klub

Gay dance club
Diskotéka pro gaye

Let's go to that downtown cabaret.
*Pojďme do toho **kabaretu** v centru města.*

Where are my chaps? I feel like hitting up the leather bar tonight.
*Kde mám chapsy? Šel bych dnes večer do **leather baru**.*

·····Alcohol
Alkohol

Beer and wine are definitely the most popular social lubricants in the Czech Republic, but they aren't the only kind. Rum? Vodka? Fernet or Becherovka? Take your pick and fill your shot glass. Or more likely, your Czech friend will choose for you and force you to try a shot whether you want to or not.

What are you drinking?
Co piješ?

Do they have booze here?
*Mají tady nějakej **chlast**?*

What are you having? It's on me.
Co si dáš? Je to na mě.

I'm buying.
Já to platím.

Another round, please!
Ještě jednu rundu, prosím!

Let's make a toast!
Připijem si!
When toasting, make sure to look everyone in the eyes. It's considered impolite not to, because it might seem like you're more interested in the booze than in their company.

Cheers!
Na zdraví!
Literally, "To your/our health."

Down the hatch!
Do dna!

Chug it!
Na ex!

I'll have…
Já si dám…

> **a rum and Coke.**
> *kolu s rumem.*
>
> **Becherovka and tonic.**
> *Beton.*
>
> **Fernet and tonic.**
> *Bavorák.*
>
> **bubbly.**
> *šampáňo.*
>
> **a Coke and red wine.**
> *houbu.*
> Don't knock it 'til you've tried it.
>
> **a nonalcoholic drink.**
> *nealko.*
> Lame-o!
>
> **soda.**
> *limonádu.*
> *Limonáda* translates as "lemonade" or any fruit-flavored soda.

Let's drink till we're…
Pijeme…

> **fucking wasted!**
> *do němoty!*
> Literally, " 'til we can't talk anymore."
>
> **dead!**
> *do mrtva!*

·····Beer
Pivo

One of the first nations to brew and enjoy beer, Czechs have been making tasty suds since 1307 when the town of Plzeň started selling their famous beer that we now know as "pilsner"—yes, as in Pilsner Urquell (*Plzeňský Prazdroj*). Another world-renowned beer name, Budweiser, has its roots in the Czech city of České Budějovice. (The German word *Budweiser* means "from Budweis," Budweis being the German name for České Budějovice, where the original Budweiser—*Budějovický budvar*—is crafted.) As many of us know by now, an American company (I won't mention any names…) exploited this name for its own weak imitation, and the original Czech Budweiser is now sold in the U.S. under the name *Czechvar*.

Golden lager
Světlý ležák
This is the typical Czech beer, commonly referred to as *světlé* (light). It's light, bitter and a little hoppy.

Dark lager
Černý ležák ; Tmavý ležák
A bit sweeter and almost black in color, this beer is also simply called *tmavý* (dark) or *černý* (black).

Cut beer
Řezané pivo
This delicious concoction, sometimes just called *řezaný*, is a mix of dark and light beers poured right from the tap.

Small one (a third-liter)
Malý

Tall one (a half-liter; a bit more than a pint)
Velký

This 10° degree beer goes down smooth!
*Tahle **desítka** se dobře pije!*
What do degrees have to do with suds? In the CR, beers come in two strengths: 10° (*desítka*) and 12° (*dvanáctka*). The 10-degree beer is lighter in taste and color, while the 12-degree one is stronger, heavier, darker and has a thick head. Mmmmm…frothy.

What the fuck, this beer tastes like piss!
*Do prdele, tohle **pivo** chutná jak chcánky!*

Hey, go get me some brews!
*Hele, dojdi mi pro **pivko**!*

Who's up for some brewskies?
*Kdo chce zajít na **pivečko**?*

It's fucking hot today, a cold one would be nice.
*Dneska je hrozný vedro, jedno **studený** by bodlo.*

Do you have any bottled beer in the fridge?
*Máš v lednici nějaký **lahvový pivo**?*

I'm getting a bottle (of beer).
*Dám si **lahváče**.*

I've only got cans in here.
*Mám tady jenom **plechovky**.*

What's on tap here?
Co se tady čepuje?

Give me two drafts, please.
Dám si dvě točený, prosím.

Wait, have one more mug with me.
Počkej, dej si se mnou ještě jeden půllitr.
Půllitr are the half-liter glass mugs used to serve draught beers.

·····Wine
Víno ; Vínko ; Vínečko

Okay, perhaps people don't always associate wines with the Czech Republic. However, the light and refreshing Czech wines are really popular there and in neighboring countries. Unfortunately, the small South Moravian and North Bohemian wineries don't produce enough grapes to for the *vínko*-guzzling natives, so a lot is imported from other parts of Europe and South America. The most popular Czech red and white varietals, such as *Rulandské modré* (Pinot Noir), *Frankovka* (Cabernet Franc), *Veltlínské zelené* (Green Veltliner) and *Tramín* (Gewurztraminer), are always worth trying. If you like Chardonnay, you should go for Muller-Thurgau.

Wine festival
Vinobraní
September is the time to visit South Moravian or North Bohemian cities and villages, where there's a *vinobraní* going on at any given moment.

Where can I find a good wine bar around here?
Kde je tady v okolí nějaká dobrá vinárna?

When are you gonna carry burčák?
Kdy budete mít burčák?
Burčák is a very young, fruity, effervescent wine made with white grapes. Only available during the fall harvest (September to November), the crisp and sweet *burčák's* pretty easy to drink—and get drunk on. Don't send your *burčák* back if you see a cloudy, yeasty liquid in your glass; it's supposed to look like that.

Mulled wine
Svařené víno ; Svařák
In the freezing cold winter, there's nothing better than hot red wine
with cinnamon, cloves, lemon and sugar. An orgasm in a cup.

We'll have a liter of red wine in a carafe.
Dáme si litr červeného v karafě.

Give us a bottle of the house white.
Dejte nám láhev domácího bílého.

All the wine cellars pour wine right from the cask.
Všechny vinné sklípky nalévají víno přímo ze sudu.

I'll have…
Já si dám…

> **a glass.**
> *sklenku.*
>
> **a two.**
> *dvojku.*
> A glass of wine is two deciliters.
>
> **a deci of wine.**
> *a decku vína.*
> Czechs dig using diminutives. They'll say, "Let's go for a
> deci of wine," even if they know they'll likely drink two liters
> with you.

•••••Hard alcohol
Tvrdý alkohol

Tired of drinking beer and wine? Don't worry, Czechs have
other ways to get you to the church of the porcelain god. *Na
zdraví* (cheers)!

Becherovka
Pale yellow in color, this herbal liqueur made from chamomile,
anise, cloves and other spices was created 200 years ago
in the spa town of Karlovy Vary and was originally used for
medicinal purposes. It's usually drunk ice-cold but can be
mixed with tonic and ice to make the bittersweet concoction
called *Beton* (translated as "concrete").

Slivovice

Do you like plums and hard booze? Then you'll probably enjoy this strong, crystal-clear plum brandy, also called *slivovitz*, that's served in small shot glasses. Czechs also use it as a home remedy for colds and sore throats. Other fruit-based Czech brandies include *meruňkovice* (apricot), *třešňovice* (cherry) and *hruškovice* (pear).

Fernet

Fernet is a dark brown, thick, bitter liqueur made in Plzeň, Czech Republic, and Trieste, Italy. It's flavored with herbs straight from the Mediterranean and Alps. *Fernet Citrus* is a sweeter version of the original. Both are served as a shot or mixed with tonic to create a drink called *Bavorák* (that's not to be confused with the Bavarian beer, though this mixture does foam like its namesake).

Tuzemák

Tuzemský rum is made from sugar beets instead of sugarcane, so it's got a deep brown color and is sweeter than your average Jamaican rum. A shot of *tuzemák* in tea garnished with lemon makes a great winter grog.

Absint

Absinthe, or the "green fairy" (although it can be blue or clear), is an intensely alcoholic, anise-flavored spirit made from a combination of herbs including wormwood leaves. It's some crazy shit. The traditional way to down this psychedelic liquid is to dip a teaspoon (or a fancy little absinthe spoon that has holes in it) with a sugar cube in a glass of absinthe and light the cube on fire. The sugar bubbles and falls in the glass, then you toss the hot liquid down the hatch.

Rum
Rum

Vodka
Vodka

Gin
Gin

Whiskey
Whisky

Tequila
Tekila

Champagne
Šampaňský

Cocktail
Koktejl

Mixed drink
Mixovaný nápoj

Let's move to something harder.
Pojď si dát něco tvrdšího.

Whoa, this Becherovka is stronger than I thought.
Aah, ta Becherovka je silnější, než jsem si myslel / myslela.

I'll have a Fernet and whiskey on the rocks.
Dám si Fernet a vizoura na led.

Make it a double.
Dám si dvojitýho.

Get a shot of slivovitz and you'll feel better.
Dej si panáka slivovice a budeš se cítit líp.

Hey, give us one more round!
Hele, dej nám ještě jednu rundu!

We gotta drink it up!
To musíme zapít!

I gotta chase this rum with a beer.
Musím toho ruma zapít pivem.

·····Drunkenness

Opilost

I'm...
Jsem...

> **a little tipsy.**
> *v náladě.*
>
> **buzzed.**
> *přiopilej / přiopilá.*
>
> **drunk.**
> *opilej / opilá.*
>
> **faded.**
> *namazanej / namazaná.*
>
> **wasted.**
> *ožralej / ožralá.*
>
> **wrecked.**
> *na šrot.*
>
> **sloppy drunk.**
> *ožralej / ožralá jak prase.*
> Literally, "drunk as a pig."
>
> **shit-faced.**
> *na sračky.*

How much did she drink?
Kolik toho vypila?

Shit, where did Josef get so wasted?
Do prdele, kde se Josef takhle ožral?

We drank everything in sight.
Vypili jsme, co jsme mohli.

Alcoholic
Alkoholik

This alkie's boozing all the time.
*Tenhle **alkáč** pořád chlastá.*

He's a regular here, just an **old drunk**.
*Je tady štamgast, jeden **starej ožrala**.*

I'm hungover.
Mám kocovinu.

I have a **splitting hangover**.
*Třeští mi **hlava**.*

I don't remember a damn thing.
Vůbec nic si nepamatuju.

He got so drunk last night he pissed himself.
Včera večer se tak vožral, že se pochcal.

Don't worry, you'll sleep it off.
Neboj, z toho se vyspíš.

What time did you pass out last night?
V kolik hodin jsi včera odpadnul?

He drank his life away.
Všechno prochlastal.

He's a first-class drunk.
Chlastá první ligu.
Literally, "He drinks the first league." It's a play on the first league
in hockey or soccer.

He's / She's a **drinking machine**.
*Je to **ochlasta / násoska**.*

My old man drank himself to death.
Můj fotr se upil k smrti.

That dude puked all over himself.
Ten frajer se celej poblil.

Man, what happened last night?
Chlape, co se včera stalo?

Dogg, I'm so embarrassed about last night.
Ty vole, po včerejšku je mi fakt trapně.

I feel like such an ass!
Cítím se jak největší kretén!

I have the spins.
Motám se.

You look like crap today. How was last night?
Vypadáš dnes hrozně. Jaký to včera bylo?

·····Refusing a drink
Odmítnutí nápoje

I'm not a drinker.
Nepiju.

Thanks, but no more.
Díky, už ne.

Shit, I don't wanna drink anymore.
Do prdele, už nic nechci pít.

Hey, stop pouring for him!
Hele, už mu nenalejvej!

I can't even look at another beer.
Už nemůžu další pivo ani vidět.

I can't take any more shots!
Už nemůžu žádný panáky!

I've had enough!
Už mám dost!

None for me, I'm driving.
Pro mě nic, já řídím.

·····Drugs
Drogy

Alcohol and cigs are like water and air for Czechs, but if you want something more intense, you can still score drugs in a lot of the bigger cities. It makes sense—after all, Amsterdam is just a car ride away. If you do decide to go for the greener or harder shit, be careful, because possession of more than the legal amount of marijuana (half an ounce) or cocaine (1 gram) can get you into jail for up to one year, and up to two years for possession of other illicit drugs.

What are you using?
Na čem jedeš?

User
Narkoman / Narkomanka

To do drugs
Fetovat

To get high
Sjet se

Junkie
Feťák / Feťačka

Addict
Závislák / Závislačka

Druggie
Toxík

Bad trip
Špatnej trip

Depression
Deprese ; Depka

Halucination
Halucinace ; Haluze

Withdrawal
Absťák

Overdose
Předávkování

OD
Přešleh

Deadly overdose
Zlatá dávka
Literally, "a golden bang."

If he doesn't stop with this shit, he'll end up in the nuthouse.
Jestli s tím svinstvem neskončí, skončí v blázinci.

He belongs in Bohnice.
Ten patří do Bohnic.
Bohnice is a notorious Czech nuthouse.

WEED
Tráva

Do you smoke…?
Kouříš…?

weed
tráva

marijuana
marihuana

Mary Jane
marjána

green
zelí
Literally, "cabbage."

pot
konopí

bud
ganja

Wanna smoke a…?
Chceš si dát…?

> **joint**
> *jointa*

> **jay**
> *spek*

> **spliff**
> *brko*

Where can I score some drugs here?
Kde tady s--Ženu nějaký drogy?

Where can I score some drugs here?
Kde tady seženu nějaký drogy?

Do you know any dealers?
Znáš nějaký dealery?

Do you have any connections?
Máš nějaké konekce?

I know he's a stoner.
Vím, že je to vyhulenec.

You look nicely baked.
Vypadáš pěkně zhulenej.

Pothead
Hašišák

Hashish
Hašiš

Hash
Haš
You may also hear hash called *čaras*, a special type used predominantly in India.

Skull hunter
Lovec lebek
A mix of hash and herb.

SMACK
Ejč

Heroin
Heroin

H
Háčko

Heron
Kedr

Brown ; White
Hnědej ; Bílej
Heroin, depending on the color and purity.

Speedball
Speedball

A knob
Šutr
Heroin in the form of a knob.

Braun
Braun ; Béčko
"Czech heroin," a drug made mostly from codein.

To shoot up
Šlehat si

To bang
Bouchat si

> **If you gonna bang, you better get a clean spike.**
> *Jestli si jdeš bouchnout, použij novou pumpu.*

Needle
Jehla

Pump
Pumpa

Banger
Buchna

COKE
Koks

Cocaine
Kokain

White powder
Bílej prach

Blow
Šňup

Snow
Sníh

I saw this junkie in the bathroom snorting snow.
Viděl jsem na záchodě toho feťáka šňupat sníh.

Dope
Matroš

Let's do lines before the concert.
Pojď si dát před koncertem lajnu.

OTHER DRUGS
Další drogy

P
Péčko

Geep
Piko

Methadone
Metadon

Meth
Pervitin

Meth addict
Perníkář

To tweak
Pikař

Tweaker
Péčkař

Crack
Krek

Crackhead
Smažka

To slam
Smažit
Literally, "to fry."

LSD
Elesdé

Acid
Kyselina

Ecstasy
Extáze

E
Éčko

E.X. rolls
Koule

Speed
Speed

Ephedrine
Efko

Morphine
Emko

Ketamin
Keťák

Diazepam
Diák

Rohypnol
Roháč

R
Erko

CHAPTER 4

BODY CZECH
TĚLESNÁ ČEŠTINA

While there never may be a Czech diet craze (have you ever tried Czech roasted duck with dumplings, cabbage and a half-liter of Pilsner?), Czechs are generally in good shape. Why? Because they always try to stay active and everyone walks everywhere. In addition, Czechs have some damn fine genes—just take a look at all the beautiful babes on the streets. Yup, ladies are smoking hot and take great pride in their appearance. They put some effort—and green—into looking good. And when I say good, I mean world-class good: Supermodels Paulina Pořizková, Daniela Peštová, Eva Herzigová and Karolina Kůrková all hail from the Czech Republic.

•••••Body
Tělo

She has a bangin' body.
Má skvělou rajcovní postavu.

She looks like a supermodel.
Vypadá jako modelka.

She has...
Má...

> amazingly **long legs**.
> *překrásný dlouhý nohy.*

> a cute **butt**.
> *pěknej zadek.*

He's...
Je...

> a total **jock**.
> *to pořádná hrana.*

> **sporty**.
> *to sportovní typ.*

> kinda short.
> *docela malej.*

He's got **chiseled abs**.
Má vypracované břišní svaly.

He's out of shape.
Nemá fyzičku.

She has a **body like a gazelle**—you'd never guess that she's 50!
Ta má tělo jak gazela—nikdy bys neřekl / neřekla, že jí je padesát!

I'm into **chubby** broads.
Jsem na ženský při těle.

He's **ripped** like Arnold.
Je namakanej jako Arnold.

I go to the gym almost every day. Wanna see my **six-pack**?
Jsem v posilovně skoro každý den. Chceš vidět můj pekáč buchet?

Renata's got kind of a **belly**.
Renata má docela bříško.

Nice **beer gut**, man.
Pěknej pivní pupek, chlape.

Check out that dude's lumberjack beard.
Mrkni na toho frajera, má fousy jak dřevorubec.

Look, that Swedish chick has the body of a linebacker.
Koukej, tahle Švédka má tělo jak almaru.

·····Body types
Tělesné typy

He / She is…
Je…

> **well fed.**
> *dobře živenej / živená.*
>
> **well built.**
> *dobře stavěnej / stavěná.*
>
> **buff.**
> *udělanej / udělaná.*
>
> **athletic.**
> *atletickej / atletická.*
>
> **ripped.**
> *namakanej / namakaná.*
>
> **muscular.**
> *svalnatej / svalnatá.*
>
> **lean.**
> *štíhlej / štíhlá.*
>
> **frail.**
> *křehkej / křehká.*
>
> **emaciated.**
> *vychrtlej / vychrtlá.*
>
> **skin and bones.**
> *kost a kůže.*
>
> **fat.**
> *tlustej / tlustá.*
>
> **obese.**
> *obézní.*
>
> **tall.**
> *vysokej / vysoká.*

small.
malej / malá.

short.
krátkej / krátká.

Hey shrimp, do you need a higher chair?
Hej skrčku, potřebuješ vyšší židli?

I'm going for that swimmer's body look.
Snažím se mít tělo jak plavec / plavkyně.

Nobody will even know if you're balding, you're a skyscraper.
Nikdo ani nepozná, že plešatíš, jakej si čahoun.

She has the body of a skeleton—you can count every one of her ribs.
Má tělo jako kostlivec—můžeš jí spočítat všechny žebra.

·····Sexy

Sexy

Here are some phrases to describe the lucky gorgeous Slavic SOBs.

He's / She's…
Je…

> **hot.**
> *to kus.*
>
>> **That hot ass is going out for dinner with me tonight.**
>> *Tenhle kus dnes večer beru na večeři.*
>
> **attractive.**
> *přitažlivej / přitažlivá.*
>
> **cute.**
> *pěknej / pěkná.*
>
> **handsome. / pretty.**
> *hezkej / hezká.*
>
> **a hottie.**
> *to hezoun / kočka.*

a beauty.
krasavec / kráska.

a stud (m.) / a stunner (fem.)
fešák / fešanda.

a muscleman / woman.
svalovec / svalovkyně.

What a bombshell!
To je ale sexbomba!

Eva likes guys with big guns.
Eva je na kluky s velkejma bicákama.

She met that hunk at the gym.
Zná toho borce z posilovny.

He / She ain't bad looking.
Nevypadá špatně.

Pepa is very good looking.
Pepa vypadá moc dobře.

Lookin' sharp!
Vypadáš bezvadně!

Damn, you're...
Ty jo, ty jsi...

> **gorgeous.**
> *nádhernej / nádherná.*
>
> **charming.**
> *okouzlující.*
>
> **a ten.**
> *jednička.*
>
> **fashionable.**
> *moderní.*
>
> **tan.**
> *opálenej / opálená.*
>
> **freckly.**
> *pihatej / pihatá.*

•••••Ugly
Ošklivej / Ošklivá

Because we can't all look like supermodel Hana Soukupová or soccer hottie Milan Baroš, and because sometimes you gotta tell it like it is.

He's / She's...
Je...

weird.
divnej / divná.

nothing much.
nic moc.

plain.
nemastnej-neslanej / nemastná-neslaná.

unattractive.
neatraktivní.

fugly.
to držka.

unkept.
zanedbanej / zanedbaná.

formless.
neforemnej / neforemná.

plump.
oplácanej / oplácaná.

soft.
rozteklej / rozteklá.

dumpy.
zavalitej / zavalitá.

husky.
obtloustlej / obtloustlá.

a fat ass.
to tlustá prdel.

as fat as a pig.
tlustá jako prase.

butt-ugly.
ošklivej / ošklivá jako prdel.

white.
bílej / bílá.

fucking pale.
bílej / bílá jak sejra.
Literally, "white as cheese."

bowlegged.
křivonohej / křivonohá.

gaunt.
vyzáblej / vyzáblá.

skeletonic.
vyzáblej / vyzáblá jako kostra.

anorexic.
anorektickej / anorektická.

disgusting.
nechutnej / nechutná.

repulsive.
odpudivej / odpudivá.

a bleached blonde.
peroxidovej blondýn / peroxidová blondýna.

a midget.
trpaslík / trpaslice.

overgrown.
přerostlej / přerostlá.

Růža went overboard on the whole bodybuilding
stint—she looks like an **Amazon** now.
*Růža to s tou kulturistikou přehnala—teď vypadá jak
Amazonka.*

You could use a bacon sandwich with mayo—you're
skinny as a twig.
*Měl / Měla by sis dát sendvič se slaninou a majonézou. Jsi
hubenej / hubená jak lunt.*

Sorry, but I don't date **beanpoles**.
*Promiň, ale nechodím s **kolohnátama**.*

Your date is totally **cross-eyed**.
*Ten kluk / ta holka, se kterým / kterou randíš pěkně **šilhá**.*

At least he's not a **four-eyes.**
*Aspoň není **šikmovokej** / **šikmovoká.***

Move it, **tubby**!
*Uhni, **otesánku**.*

Her ass is as **big as a house.**
*Má prdel **jako stodolu**.*
Literally, "barn."

What a **lard-ass.**
*To je ale **tlustoprd** / **tlustoprdka**.*

I can't look at him, he's **hideous.**
*Nemůžu se na něj ani podívat, **je šerednej**.*

Miloš made one too many visits to the tanning salon—
he looks like a **lobster.**
*Miloš to přehnal s opalováním v solárku a teď vypadá jak
spařený prase.*
Literally, "steamed pig."

He's / She's got…
On / Ona má…

> a big **honker.**
> *velkej **frňák**.*

> a **schnoz.**
> *nos jako skobu.*
> Literally, "a nose like a hook."

> a double chin.
> *dvojitou bradu.*

> a hunchback.
> *hrb jako velbloud.*
> Literally, "a hump like a camel."

> Mickey Mouse ears.
> *uši jako Mickey-Mouse.*

> a spare tire.
> *pneumatiky.*

> beaver teeth.
> *zuby jak vydra.*

huge lips.
obrovský rty.

a Mick Jagger mouth.
velkou tlamu.
Literally, "big muzzle."

·····Illness
Nemoc

We all feel shitty sometimes. Especially after a long night of drinking beers and Becherovka shots then stuffing our faces with pub kielbasas, sausages and headcheese.

What's wrong with you?
Co je s tebou?

I'm…
Jsem…

tired as a dog.
utahanej / utahaná jak pes.

worn out.
hotovej / hotová.

I'm not so hot today.
Dneska se necítím nejlíp.

I feel…
Je mi…

nauseous.
nevolno.

kinda yucky.
docela blbě.

really shitty.
fakt na hovno.

I'd be better off dead.
Radši bych umřel / umřela.

You're pale as a sheet.
Jseš bledej / bledá jako stěna.
Literally, "pale as a wall."

You look like crap!
Vypadáš mizerně!

My stomach's churning and my head is pounding.
Zvedá se mi žaludek a třeští mi hlava.
Literally, "my stomach is lifting."

I have...
Mám...

> **a migraine.**
> *migrénu.*

> **a fever.**
> *horečku.*

> **the flu.**
> *chřipku.*

> **strep throat.**
> *angínu.*

> **stomach cramps.**
> *křeče v břiše.*

> **heartburn.**
> *pálí mě žáha.*

I've got the shakes.
Celej / Celá se třesu.

Do you have...?
Máš...?

> **antacids**
> *antacida*

> **aspirin**
> *acylpirin*

> **Ibuprofen**
> *brufen*

> **cough drops**
> *kapky na kašel*

> **a decongestant**
> *něco proti rýmě*

> **antibiotics**
> *antibiotika*

a Band-Aid
náplast

Not in the ass, I have hemmorhoids!
Do zadku ne, mám hemeroidy!

I wanna barf everytime I look at her.
Chce se mi blít, když jí vidím.

She vomited all over his jeans.
Pozvracela mu džíny.

I puked my guts out.
Vyzvracel jsem se z podoby.

Move, gotta hurl!
Uhni, musím hodit šavli!
Literally, "throwing the sword."

Lumír was praying to the porcelain god all night.
Lumír celou noc objímal mísu.
Literally, "hugging the bowl."

·····Pissing
Chcaní

Public restrooms in the Czech Republic are usually in decent shape because you gotta "pay to spray." In most big-city metro, bus and train stations, the restrooms have their very own washroom attendants. Yep, be ready to shed some extra dough for a few squares of toilet paper (about 5 crowns). Even the men's rooms have female attendants (usually the angry, mean grandma type), so don't be surprised when an angry, mean grandma decides to tidy up the main bathroom just as you're emptying your bladder. Just ignore her and try to finish the job. If the facilities are spotless and the attendants are nice, don't forget to tip them a few *Kč*. For those of you who'd rather not be pampered while on the pot, you certainly can and will find some shittier places with piss walls. Yeah, these are exactly what you'd imagine—walls where water and urine are constantly trickling down, creating the most unbelievably rank smell. So if you're picky about where you piss, choose wisely.

Bathroom attendant
Toaletář / Toaletářka

I gotta…
Musím…

> **go number one.**
> *na malou.*
>
> **urinate.**
> *močit.*
>
> **pee-pee.**
> *se vyčůrat.*
>
> **take a leak.**
> *se vymočit.*
>
> **take a piss.**
> *se vychcat.*
>
> **mark my territory.**
> *to tady označkovat.*

Blanka laughed so hard she tinkled in her panties.
Blanka se tak smála, až si ucvrnkla do kalhotek.

I almost whizzed myself laughing.
Málem jsem se pochcal smíchy.

I bet I can piss farther than you.
Vsaď se, že dochčiju dál než ty.

I gotta pee in the bushes.
Musím se vyčůrat tady v křoví.

It smells like piss in here.
Smrdí to tady jak chcánky.

·····Shitting
Sraní

Czech speakers generally don't discuss crapping, urinating or
other bodily functions as often and as eagerly as potty-mouth
Americans do. Everyone shits, right? So why get all worked
up about it?

I gotta…
Musím…

> **go to the toilet.**
> *na záchod.*
>
> **go number two.**
> *na velkou.*
>
> **poop.**
> *kakat.*
>
> **shit.**
> *srát.*
>
> **take a shit.**
> *se vysrat.*
>
> > **Nothing better than taking a good shit!**
> > *Není nad to se pořádně vysrat!*
>
> **drop a turd.**
> *položit kabel.*
> Literally, "lay a cable."

wipe my ass.
si vytřít prdel.

I...
Mám...

am constipated.
zácpu.

have diarrhea.
průjem.

have the runs.
sračku.

have the shits.
sračku jako bič.
Literally, "runs like a whip."

Yesterday I was, like, peeing outta my butt.
Včera jsem chcal / chcala prdelí.

I almost crapped my pants.
Málem jsem si nasral / nasrala do kalhot.

I shit myself.
Vysral / Vysrala jsem se z podoby.
Literally, "I shat myself out of my visage."

It smells awful!
To je ale smrad!

You're a real stinker!
Ty jsi ale smraďoch / smraďoška!

Flush it! I don't wanna see your shit!
Spláchni to! Nechci vidět tvý hovno!

·····Farting
Prdění

Uhhh...Who farted in here?
Fuj... Kdo si tady prdnul?

My fart just ripped my pants.
*Ten **prd** mi roztrhnul kalhoty.*

He / She let one rip.
Uprdnul / Uprdla si.

Someone just dropped an atomic bomb.
*Někdo vypustil **atomovku**.*

Hold your breath, I'm gonna let a ghost out.
*Zadrž dech, **vypustím ducha**.*

He's / She's a nasty farter.
*Je to **prďoch / prďoška**.*

Klára let out a silent fart.
*Klára vypustila **tichošlápka**.*

Man, you smell like a skunk!
*Ty vole, smrdíš jako **tchoř**!*
A tchoř is a fitch (or polecat) that doesn't actually spray stinky stuff, but does have a funky smell.

·····Other bodily functions and fluids

Další tělesné funkce a tekutiny

My grandma snores like a chain saw.
*Moje babička **chrápe** jak motorová pila.*

Dominik grinds his teeth in his sleep.
*Dominik ve spaní **skřípe zubama**.*

I got a cramp in my left leg.
*Mám **křeč** v levé noze.*

She's preggers.
*Je v **jináči**.*

Vašek knocked her up.
*Vašek jí **zbouchnul**.*

Earwax
Ušní maz

I have a runny nose.
Teče mi z nosu.
Literally, "my nose is leaking."

Snot
Nudle

> **Wipe up your snot.**
> *Utři si tu nudli.*

Yuck! Don't blow your nose on your hand.
Fuj! Nesmrkej si do ruky.

Dude, quit picking your nose.
Frajere, přestaň se rejpat v nose.

Stop drooling over her, she's my girl!
Přestaň slintat, to je moje holka!

I saw you eat your boogers.
Viděl jsem tě jíst holuby z nosu.
Literally, "pigeons from your nose."

You have eyeboogers, sleepyhead.
Máš ospalky, ospalče.

Everyone gets blackheads now and then.
Každýmu se sem tam udělaj beďary.

Can I pop your zits?
Můžu ti vymačkat uhry?

Šárka has a lot of pimples.
Šárka má hodně pupínků.

I got my period.
Mám měsíčky.

Laura's on the rag.
Lura to zrovna má.

Where can she buy some pads?
Kde si může koupit vložky?

Do you have an extra tampon?
Máš extra tampon?

CHAPTER 5

HORNY CZECH
NADRŽENÁ ČEŠTINA

People in the Czech Republic are pretty liberal about sex (this is one of the first countries to air evening weather reports delivered by seminude women, with female viewers requesting naked male weather anchors, too—they got their wish, by the way). In fact, "soft" nudity (breasts, bare butts) is common on TV even during the day. Furthermore, premarital sex is standard—a good way to test out a potential partner's sex skills (who wants to marry someone who's bad in bed?). So if you're interested in a little something something, just ask— nobody's going to take offense. And you just might get lucky.

·····Fucking
Šukání

Are you as horny as I am?
Jsi taky tak nadrženej / nadržená?

Let's...
Pojď...

> **make love.**
> *se pomilovat.*

copulate.
souložit.

have sex.
na to skočit.

fuck.
šukat.
If you want to be even more vulgar, it's *mrdat* for you.

have a fuck.
si zašukat.

screw.
píchat.

hump.
šoustat.

have a quickie.
si dát rychlovku.

have a fuckathlon.
si dát šukatlon.

have a fuckfest.
si dát šoustanici.

We banged like crazy this morning.
Dnes ráno jsme si to pořádně rozdali.

I'm totally hot for you.
Totálně mě rajcuješ.

She wants you. Why don't you sleep with her?
Ta tě chce. Proč se s ní nevyspíš?

I'm crazy for you.
Jsem do tebe blázen.

Let's go back to my place.
Pojď ke mě domů.

Do it to me hard.
Pořádně mi to udělej.

Nail me right now!
Strč mi ho tam hned teď!

Fuck my brains out!
Pořádně mě vymrdej!

Marek claims he's gonna give it to her in the ass tonight.
Marek tvrdí, že jí ho dnes večer strčí do zadku.

He needs to get his rocks off.
Potřebuje si vylejt koule.

He's a good…
Je to dobrej…

> **screw.**
> *píchač.*
> Literally, "sticks."

> **lay.**
> *nabíječ.*
> Literally, "loader."

> **fuck.**
> *šuk / šukna.*

Those two hump like bunnies!
Ty dva šoustají jak králíci!

Radek popped her cherry and now she won't stop calling him.
Radek jí odpanil a teď mu pořád volá.

Dana's frigid but whores around all the time.
Dana je frigidní, ale kurví se pořád.

•••••Sexual positions
Sexuální pozice

I'm tired of…
Už mě nudí…

> **foreplay.**
> *předehra.*

> **French kissing.**
> *francouzáky.*

titty-fucking.
šukání mezi kozy.

finger-banging.
prstění.

missionary.
misionář.

standing T.
na stojáka.

Let's try…
Pojď zkusit…

doggy-style.
na sraba.
Literally, "the quitter's way."

through the backdoor.
do zadečku.

from the rear.
zezadu.

the wheelbarrow.
trakař.

both legs up. (the guy holds the girl's ankles up with his hands)
na cibulku.
Literally, "onion."

cowgirl.
na koníčka.

69.
šedesátdevítku.

double penetration.
dvojitou penetraci.

S & M.
sado-maso.

B & D.
zotročení a disciplínu.

anal sex.
anál.

group sex.
grupáč.

Our neighbor is strange; he might be a sadist freak.
Náš soused je divnej, je to asi sadista.

How about a threesome?
Co takhle švédská trojka?

·····Cock
Péro

Like the majority of the world, Czech dudes are uncut. And like *everywhere* in the world, there are a gazillion pet names for a guy's Johnson.

Suck my...
Kuř mi...

Jerk off my...
Hoň mi...

Spank my...
Poplácej mi...

Bite my...
Kousej mi můj / moje...

privates.
přirození.

penis.
penis. ; úd.

pecker.
pták.
Literally, "bird."

dick.
vocas.
Literally, "tail."

tool.
nářadí.

Every chick in Brno knows that your cousin is hung.
Každá buchta v Brně ví, že tvůj bratranec ho má velkýho.

A COCKFEST)))
PŘEHLÍDKA VOCASŮ

Rod
Kláda

Prick
Čurák

Trouser snake
Hadice

Sausage
Klobása

Weiner
Párek

Gear
Nádobíčko

Giant redwood
Pořádná kláda
Literally, "a hell of a log."

Erect penis
Ztopořenej penis

Boner
Tvrdý péro

Limp dick
Povislý ; Zvadlý péro

Wee-wee
Bimbas

Little prick
Čuráček

Johnson
Piňdour

Toothpick
Párátko

Head
Žalud

Cut cock
Obřezaný péro

Uncut cock
Neobřezaný péro

He's packing a 10-incher.
Má ho čtvrt-metrovýho.
Literally, "a quarter of a meter" (25 centimeters). It's that whole
metric system thing everyone else in the world uses.

Have you ever seen a foreskin this big?
Už jsi někdy viděl / viděla takhle velkou předkožku?

Hey, I didn't know you were cut!
Hele, nevěděl / nevěděla jsem, že máš vobřízku!

Can I stick it in your ass?
Můžu ti ho strčit do zadku?

I think he's impotent.
Myslím, že je impotentní.

·····Balls
Koule

I hate when you squeeze my balls.
Nesnáším, když mi mačkáš koule.

We smashed so hard my balls hurt.
Prcali jsme tak zvostra, až mě bolí koule.

Grab my...
Chyť mě za...

Suck my...
Cucej mi...

> **scrotum.**
> *šourek.*
>
> **testicles.**
> *varlata.*
>
> **ball sac.**
> *pytel.*

Lick my...
Lízej moje...

package.
nádobíčko.

family jewels.
rodinné klenoty.

nuts.
vejce.
Literally, "eggs."

Karel is proud of his low-hangers.
*Karel je moc pyšnej na svoje **povislé koule**.*

·····Cock action
Péro v akci

Jack off
Onanovat

I'm just gonna watch porn at home and jack off.
*Budu se doma dívat na porno a **onanovat**.*

Jerk off
Honit si ho

Have you jerked off today?
*Už sis **ho** dnes **vyhonil**?*

If I don't score any chick tonight, I'll just have to…
Jestli dneska nesbalím žádnou buchtu, budu si muset…

choke the chicken.
vyhonit ptáka.
Literally, "chase the bird."

buff the banana.
vymastit lano.
Literally, "grease the rope."

beat the meat.
vyhonit vocas.
Literally, "hunt the tail."

Give me 5 minutes, I'm masturbating right now.
*Dej mi 5 minut, zrovna **masturbuju**.*

Come on, give me a blow job!
Tak dělej, vykuř mi ho!

Erika gives great head.
Erika skvěle kouří.
Literally, "Erika smokes great."

Does Anna smoke? She smokes but doesn't swallow.
Anna kouří? Ona kouří, ale nepolyká.
This is a pretty common joke in the CR. "Smoking" refers to both smoking cigarettes or giving blow jobs, so be careful when you ask if a girl smokes cigarettes—you might get a cold reception, or quite the opposite.

Jordan is a masturbating machine.
Jordan je onanista / onanistka.

I'm gonna shove it right into her mouth.
Strčím jí ho rovnou do pusy.

She always wants me to dick-slap her face.
Vždycky chce, abych jí plácal ptákem po obličeji.

·····Boobs and ass
Prsa a zadek

If you're a titty-lover visiting the Czech Republic anytime from May to late September (when the weather's warm), you're in for a treat. Czech girls love to go braless beneath a thin T-shirt or see-through summer dress. Enjoy, you lucky motherfucker!

Can I touch your...?
Můžu ti šáhnout na...?

Can I suck on your...?
Můžu ti cucat...?

Can I stick it between your...?
Můžu ti ho strčit mezi...?

> **boobies**
> *prsíčka*

tits
kozy

jugs
měchy
Literally, "bellows."

bagpipes
dudy

honkers
nárazníky

melons
melouny

fake boobs
silikony

Nice...
Pěkný...

You have great...
Máš skvělý...

nipples.
bradavky.

erect nipples.
dudlíky.

headlights.
rádia.

huge tits.
kozy jako vozy.
Literally, "goats as wagons."

balloons.
balóny.

Dana is a **bra-buster**.
*Dana je **prsatice**.*

I've never seen such a big **boulder holder**!
*Nikdy jsem neviděl větší **padáky**!*

I adore your **small titties**.
*Zbožňuju tvoje **kůzlátka**.*
Literally, "kids" or "young goats."

She's got no breasts.
Nemá žádný prsa.

She's as flat as an ironing board.
Je plochá jak žehlící prkno.

I'm in love with…
Miluju…

> **your butt.**
> *tvůj zadek.*
>
> **your booty.**
> *tvůj zadeček.*
>
> **your butthole.**
> *tvou prdel.*
>
> **your rump.**
> *tvoje šunky.*
> Literally, "hams."
>
> **your junk in the trunk.**
> *tvojí oplácanou zadnici.*
>
> **your derriere.**
> *tvůj výstřih.*
>
> **your butt cheeks.**
> *tvoje půlky.*
>
> **your ass crack.**
> *tvoji řiťku.*

She has an ass like a barn!
Ta má prdel jako stodolu!
Use this phrase when you want to rough it up.

Her little ass looks like it's made from porcelain.
Má prdelku jak z porcelánu.
In other words, firm, smooth and nicely rounded…

Sandra's totally assless.
Sandra nemá žádnej zadek.

Can I lick your asshole?
Můžu ti lízat čokodíru?

·····Pussy

Pička

My…is so wet!
Moje…je úplně vlhká!

vagina
vagina

cooch
číča

coochie
micina

hole
díra

cunt
kunda

twat
píča

slit
štěrbina

Your…makes me so horny!
Tvoje…mě pořádně rajcuje!

clam
mušle

pussy juice
šťáva ; šťavka

shaved pussy
letiště
Literally, "airport." There might not be a landing strip at this airport—it's usually clean shaven.

beaver
bobr

bush
křoví

clit
poštěváček

I'm completely shaved.
Jsem celá vyholená.

Find my G-spot and finger me!
Najdi můj G-bod a vyprsti mě!

My pussy has been on fire all day—I wanna feel you
inside me.
Celý den mě svrbí pička, chci tě cítit v sobě.
Literally, "My pussy has been itching for you."

Damn, she has a huge forest down there!
Ty jo, ta má pořádnej prales tam dole! ; ...boubín...
Boubín refers to the Boubín prales, a primeval forest in Bohemia.

Can I smell your pubes?
Můžu si čichnout k tvému ochlupení?

Show me your garden.
Ukaž mi zahrádku.

Can I shave it?
Můžu ti jí oholit?

·····Let's get it on!
Jdem na to!

I'm sure many of you horndogs have heard of (or at least seen)
Jana Cova, Stacy Silver, Tim Hamilton or Johan Volny—the
stage names of Czech porn stars with worldwide recognition.
Not everyone can look like a porn star, but we can all talk, kiss,
fuck or at least moan like them. Here are some useful phrases
when things are heating up.

Be gentle, I'm still a virgin.
Jemně, jsem ještě panic / panna.

You're getting me all excited!
Fakt mě vzrušuješ!

I've had a hard-on since this morning.
Stojí mi už od rána.

I got a boner that won't quit.
Pořád mi stojí péro.
Literally, "My cock is standing."

Let me slide it in already.
Už mě ho tam nech strčit.

You're so big and hard.
Máš ho tak velkýho a tvrdýho.

I'm all wet.
Jsem celá vlhká.

I want it inside me.
Chci tě v sobě.

Faster! Harder!
Přidej! Pořádně!

God, I'm gonna cum!
Bože, já už se udělám!

Are you almost there?
Už budeš?

Cum inside me!
Udělej se do mě!

Have you cum yet?
Už si se udělal / udělala?

I'm gonna jizz…
Nastříkám ti to…

Can I shoot it…?
Můžu ti to stříknout…?

> **in your mouth**
> *do pusy*
>
> **on your ass**
> *na zadek*
>
> **on your breasts**
> *na prsa*

on your face
na obličej

My girl always has multiple orgasms.
Moje holka se vždycky udělá několikrát za sebou.

I wanna taste your jizz.
Chci ochutnat tvojí mrdku.

She's never seen so much sperm in her life.
V životě ještě neviděla tolik sperma.

Can you get it up again?
Postaví se ti ještě?

Are you still good to go?
Ještě pořád můžeš?

Hell yeah, let's go two more times!
Že váháš, ještě dvakrát!

I can't anymore.
Už nemůžu.

My cock is empty now.
Už mám prázdný péro.

·····Sexcessories and sex obsessions
Sexuální nástroje a sexuální posedlosti

Hand me a...
Podej mi...

> **condom.**
> *kondom.*
>
> **rubber.**
> *gumu.*
>
> **raincoat.**
> *pláštěnku.*
>
> **jizz glove.**
> *šprcku.*

strap-on.
připínací robertek.

dildo.
robertka.

vibrator.
vibrátor.

butt-plug.
anální kolík.

mask.
masku.

whip.
bičík.

collar.
obojek.

Do you have some…
Máš nějaké…

    lube?
    mazadlo?

    lubricant?
    lubrikant?

WHY DOES EVERYBODY THINK I'M A...?)))
PROČ SI KAŽDEJ MYSLÍ, ŽE JSEM...?

call boy / girl
kluk / holka na zavolání

gigolo
gigolo

tramp (fem.)
lehká holka

prostitute
prostitut / prostitutka

slut
štětka

hooker
šlapka

whore
kurva

bitch
čubka

pimp
pasák

horndog
nadrženec

nymphomaniac
nymfoman / nymfomanka

fetishist
fetišista

pedophile
pedofil

voyeur
čumil

Ben Wa balls?
Venušiny kuličky?

handcuffs?
želízka?

I'm not into…
Nejsem na…

bondage.
svazování.

spanking.
výprasky.

water sports.
vodní sporty.

scat.
kaviár.

From now on I'm your Dominatrix.
Od teď jsem tvá Domina.

You will obey my command!
Budeš plnit, co ti přikážu!

You're my slave and I'm your master!
Jsi můj sluha a já tvůj Pán!

Be strict with me.
Buď na mě přísnej / přísná.

Punish me.
Potrestej mě.

Karla likes it rough.
Karla to má ráda natvrdo.

Whip me!
Zbičuj mě!

Who the fuck are you in bed?
Kdo do prdele jseš, v posteli?

·····Sexual interests
Sexuální zájmy

Do you like men or women?
Jsi na chlapy nebo na ženský?

Do you sleep with girls or boys?
Spíš s holkama nebo s klukama?

I'm into…
Jsem na…

> **women.**
> *ženský.*
>
> **men.**
> *na chlapy.*
>
> **both.**
> *obojí.*
>
> **trannies.**
> *transky.*

I'm straight.
Jsem heterák / heteračka.

I'm homosexual.
Jsem homosexuál / homsexuální.

Kurt's a homo.
Kurt je homouš.

I'm a lesbian.
Jsem lesba.

I bet that he's / she's bi.
Vsadím se, že je bisexuální.

Gay
Gay

Queer
Queer ; Buzík

Fruit
Teplouš

Fag
Buk

Woodpecker
Kuřbuřt

Fudge-packer
Čokodíra

Faggot
Buzna

Fairy
Bukvice

Butt pirate
Bukanýr

Lipstick lesbian
Lesbička

CHAPTER 6

ANGRY CZECH
naštvaná čeština

Sure, Czechs swear, but they don't seem to curse as often or as loudly as some other short-tempered nations around the world. If you really get pissed and start screaming at someone in public, you can rest assured that within seconds, you'll attract a crowd of "concerned" nosebags.

When you hear people swear on buses and trains, they're usually just muttering something like *Ježiš Marja* (Jesus Mary), *Pane Bože*! (my God!) or *do prdele* (shit) under their breath. But if you try to bitch slap a taxi driver or some drunk at a pub, you're never gonna hear the end of it. In fact, you'll hear a lot of "it" very clearly.

·····You talkin' to me?
To mluvíš se mnou?

What's up?
Co je?

Whatta ya want?
Co chceš?

What the hell is going on here?
Co se to tady sakra děje?

Watch out!
Bacha!

Say it again!
Řekni to ještě jednou!

Watch your mouth, dude.
Dej si bacha, co říkáš, frajere.

Hey buddy, you got a problem?
Hele kámo, máš nějakej problém?

Are you trying to piss me off?
Snažíš se mě nasrat?

GO TO THE ASS!)))
JDI DO PRDELE!

The most widely used phrase to show someone you're a little or a lot annoyed with them is *Jdi do prdele* (literally, "Go to the ass"). It has several meanings, depending on your intonation:

C'mon! You know I didn't mean it!
Di do prdele! Víš, že sem to tak nemyslel/nemyslela!
A "give me a break" apology.

Stop bothering me, I'm watching TV now.
Jdi do prdele, teď koukám na televizi.
Annoyance, like a fly that keeps buzzing in your face.

Screw you! I didn't want to be on your team anyway.
Jdi do prdele! Stejně jsem nechtěl / nechtěla být v tvým týmu.

Are you kidding me, the cops wreck my car and I have to pay for the damage!?
Do prdele, poldové mi nabořili auto a já musím platit škodu!?
An expression of disbelief and extreme irritation.

Fuck you!
Jdi do prdele!
I'm pissed and I really mean it so get the fuck out of my face.

You must be fucking kidding me!
To si ze mě děláš prdel!
Literally, "You must be making an ass of me."

Come on, I'm just joking.
No tak, já si jenom dělám srandu.

I'm tellin' ya, don't mess with me.
Ti řikám, nezahrávej si se mnou.

I'm not playing, asshole!
Nebudu se s tebou mazlit, hajzle!
Literally, "I'm not going to fondle you, asshole!"

·····Pissed off
Nasranej / Nasraná

When you just can't keep your comments about someone to yourself…

I can't…
Nemůžu…

> **stand you.**
> *tě vystát.*
>
> **bear the sight of him / her.**
> *se na něj / ní ani podívat.*
>
> **put up with them anymore.**
> *se už s nima babrat.*

His / Her attitude…
Jeho / Její chování…

His / Her screaming…
Jeho / Její vřískot…

His / Her shitface…
Jeho / Její vožralá držka…

> **is too much for me.**
> *je už na mě moc.*

gets on my nerves.
mi jde na nervy.

bugs the hell out of me.
mě už fakt sere.

is annoying.
mě štve.

Did you see how she busted his balls?
Viděl si, jak ho zjebala?

Stop bugging her, dude!
Přestaň jí votravovat, frajere!

Stop harassing me!
Přestaň se do mě navážet!

Shut it!
Zklapni!

Shut your piehole!
Drž klapačku!

Give me a break!
Dej mi pokoj!

Let me be!
Nech mě bejt!

I hate you.
Nesnáším tě.

·····Get out of my face!

Jdi mi z očí!
Literally, "Get out of my sight."

Go away!
Jdi pryč!

Get out of here!
Vypadni odsud!

Piss off!
Zmiz!

Back the fuck up!
Dej si vodstup, kurva!

Czech speakers also have a few interesting and more involved phrases to tell you off:

Climb on my hunchback!
Vlez mi na hrb!

Go stuff yourself!
Jdi se vycpat!

Shit your eye out!
Vyser si voko!

I've had it up to here with you!
*Už tě mám **až po krk**!*
Literally, "up to my throat."

Mind your own business!
Hleď si svýho!

Your stupid face makes me wanna puke.
Je mi z toho tvýho ksichtu na blití.

Drop dead, you freak!
Chcípni, ty zrůdo!

Get the fuck outta here!
Vypadni odsud, sakra!

·····Fuck off!

Odprejskni!

When you're dealing with annoying strangers, you never know how long it's going to be before someone's about to lose their shit and smack you right on the spot. Then there are those assholes who are all shit-talk and no action. Use these phrases at your own risk.

Go fuck yourself!
Jdi do píči!
Literally, "Go to the pussy."

I don't give a fuck.
Je mi to u prdele.
Literally, "It's near my ass."

Screw you!
Jdi do hajzlu!

Fuck no!
Kurva ne!

Fucking fuck you!
Mrdám tě!

I've fucking had it with you!
Mám tě už kurva dost!

Fucking shit!
Hovno zkurvený!

Shut the fuck up!
Drž kurva hubu!

Fuck that shit!
Mrdej na to!

Step the fuck away!
Uhni kurva!

You fucking SOB!
Ty zmrde zkurvenej!

You fucking cow!
Ty krávo zasraná!

When you call a Czech woman a *kráva* (cow), it's like calling your friend or enemy a bitch. But it's not always negative—just like in the U.S., some teen girls use this expression jokingly when talking to each other.

Kick the fucking bitch out!
Vykopni tu děvku zkurvenou!

·····Talking shit
Kecat kraviny

Czechs love some ass-slang: They don't fuck their enemies, they shit on them!

Shit!
Do prdele!

I shit on…
Seru na…

> **you.**
> *tebe.*
>
> **my nagging girlfriend—let's have a beer!**
> *mojí otravnou přítelkyni—pojď na pivo!*
>
> **my boring job—I'm gonna enjoy my life.**
> *mojí nudnou práci—budu si užívat života.*

my mean boss—he/she can say whatever he wants.

mojeho zlýho šéfa/šéfovou—ať si říká, co chce.

my lame neighbors—let's have a fucking party!

moje vadný sousedy—uděláme si skvělej mejdan!

If you don't love me, then **kiss your own ass**!

Když mě nemiluješ, tak si polib prdel!

Lick my ass!

Vyliž mi prdel!

Shit on him if he's cheating on you.

Vyser se na něj, když tě podvádí.

If you can't lend me the green, then **shove it up your ass**!

Když mi nemůžeš pučit ty prachy, tak si je strč do prdele!

Robert is always **full of shit**.

Robert furt kecá kraviny.

He / She thinks he's / she's a **badass** because he / she has an expensive motorcycle.

Myslí si, že je borec / borkyně, protože má drahou motorku.

What a **pain in the ass**!

To je ale prudič / prudička!

You really thought I was serious, you **fool**?!

Ty sis fakt myslel, že to myslím vážně, ty hlupáku?!

What an **asshole**!

No to je ale hajzl!

Don't believe it, it's **bullshit**.

Nevěř tomu, je to hovadina.

He / She does everything **half-assed**.

Dělá všechno na půl.

·····Don't be stupid!

Nebuď blbej!

Don't be such a...
Nebuď takovej...

Sometimes I think he's / she's a complete...
Někdy si myslím, že je totální...

> **dumbass.**
> *hlupák.*
>
> **dummy.**
> *blbeček.*
>
> **kiss-ass.**
> *vlezdoprdelka.*
>
> **lost case.**
> *ztracenej případ.*
>
> **loser.**
> *ubožák / ubožačka.*
>
> **moron.**
> *debil.*
>
> **retard.**
> *magor.*
>
> **freak.**
> *zrůda.*
>
> **dumb-fuck.**
> *pamrd.*
>
> **fuckup.**
> *zmrd.*
>
> **fucking zero.**
> *naprostá nula.*
>
> **jerk.**
> *pitomec.*

You're such a...
Ty jsi takovej/taková...

> **douche-bag.**
> *trapák.*

shithead.
sráč.

sucker.
cucák.

fucker.
zmrďák.

Mongoloid.
mongol.

frozen pussy.
zmrzlá píča.

fish cunt.
kunda z ryby.

Watch your ass, he's / she's weird.
Dávej si bacha, je divnej / divná.

C'mon, jump already, don't be a wimp!
Tak už skoč, nebuď srab!

·····Kick ass
Nakopat prdel

When words just aren't cuttin' it and you want to get across the message that you're not fucking around, here are some phrases to spit out between punches.

Stop with the shit about my girl / boy!
Přestaň s těma kecama o mojí holce / mým klukovi!

You're asking for a beatdown, sucker!
Ty si koleduješ o nakládačku, cucáku!

Do you want a smackdown?
Chceš, abych ti jednu natáhnul / natáhla?

I'm about to lose it!
Už se neudržím!

I'm gonna punch him in his face!
Dám mu do držky!

I'm gonna fuck you up!
Já tě ztřískám!

He whooped him good!
Pěkně ho zflákal!

You want me to rearrange your face?
Chceš, abych ti srovnal/srovnala obličej?

I'm gonna kick...
Nakopu...

> **you in the nuts!**
> *ti koule!*

> **your ass!**
> *ti prdel!*

> **your piehole!**
> *ti hubu!*

I'm gonna crack your balls wide open!
Rozkopu ti koule na kaši!

I'll tear you up!
Roztrhnu tě jak hada!

Watch out for his uppercut!
Bacha na toho zdviháka!

Bring it on!
Pojď na férovku!

Let's take it outside!
Rozdáme si to venku!
You can use this when fighting or fucking, so be careful with your tone...

They pounded the shit out of each other—the big guy busted his nose.
Mlátili se jak koně—ten vazoun mu rozbil nos.

I never wanna see you here again. Got it?
Už tě tady nikdy nechci vidět. Rozumíš?

Next time I'll kill you!
Příště tě zabiju!

⋯⋯Chill out!
Klídek!

And if you wanna be a peacemaker, not a fighter…

Yo, it's all right.
Hele, je to v pohodě.

Calm down!
Uklidni se!

Excuse me, I think you need to just mellow out right now.
Promiň, ale myslím, že by ses měl / měla zklidnit.

I'm not getting involved.
Nebudu se do toho míchat.

He doesn't have anything to do with it.
On s tím nemá nic společnýho.

It's not worth it.
Nestojí to za to.

Fuck it!
Ser na to!

Enough already!
To stačí!

Break it up, guys.
Nechte toho, kluci.

Come to your senses, gentlemen!
Mějte rozum, pánové!

It really **ain't that big a deal.**
Není to zas až tak vážný.

Let's just forget about it!
Prostě na to zapomenem!

Stay out of this!
Nepleť se do toho!

Cool it, man!
Zklidni se chlape!

Call the…
Zavolej…

> **cops.**
> *poldy.*
>
> **pigs.**
> *švestky.*
> Literally, "plums," because they wear blue uniforms and they
> look like, well, plums.
>
> **fuzz.**
> *fízly.*
>
> **ambulance.**
> *sanitku.*

CHAPTER 7

POPPY CZECH

HIP ČESKY

Czechs have come a long way since communism fell in 1989. And while the typical Czech is a little brainy and sort of patriotic, there's no escaping the overwhelming influence of the modern media craze of television and the almighty Internet. What's hot and happening in the U.S.—and the world—is usually also hot in the Czech Republic. So don't be surprised when your Czech lover dumps you through Facebook or Tweets all the juicy details of when you screwed his best friend.

·····TV

Televize

Czechs watch a lot of TV. Whether their getting ready for work in the morning, cooking dinner, sipping some brewskis at the pub or hanging out with friends, there's usually a TV on (at least in the background). So there's lots to choose from when it comes to the boob tube. Privately owned TV Nova and TV Prima draw the most viewers. But public *Česká televize* (Czech TV), which runs four different stations (ČT1, ČT2, ČT4, ČT24), is definitely more popular in the Czech Republic than PBS is in America.

If you get dizzy by flipping through all the domestic channels, don't worry—you can catch almost any cable or satellite TV you're used in the U.S.

ČT1

This family oriented channel shows Czech movies, soaps, miniseries and children's programs, including *Večerníček*, an iconic children's miniseries that has been part of Czech (and Slovakian) kids' bedtimes forever (it airs when the rugrats should be going to sleep). It's short (about ten minutes), sweet (usually animated fairytales) and beloved (so don't fucking make fun of it).

Události

Every country has it—the evening news. This one's aired at 7 p.m. and is taken pretty seriously. Don't interrupt anyone watching the program; you'll probably be shushed and ignored.

Branky, Body, Vteřiny—BBV

American sports fanatics watch *SportsCenter*; Czechs have *Branky, Body, Vteřiny* (Goals, Points, Seconds). It's ten times shorter, so you don't have to make a big commitment to watch it. And unlike its American counterpart, you get coverage of *kolová* (bicycle soccer) and *nohejbal* (foot tennis). How cool is that?

ČT2

Science, entertainment, history and nature programs, as well as major sports events and classic foreign films with subtitles rather than dubbing. Similar to PBS.

ČT4

All sports, all the time.

ČT24

Twenty-four-hour headline news. Your Czech CNN.

TV Nova

TV Nova is owned by an American conglomerate, so you'll see tons of dubbed U.S. network programs (*CSI*, *Law & Order: SVU*, *Lost*). Czech shows include *Snídaně s NOVOU* ("Breakfast with Nova," a hipper, funnier version of *Good Morning America* hosted by hotties of both the male and female persuasion) and *Ulice* ("The Street," a never-ending soap about the lives of several modern families living in the suburbs of Prague). This network is also known for *Počasíčko*, a weather show that featured forecasts seriously reported by sexy babes (mostly former Miss Czech Republic contestants and models). Who were nearly naked. Yes, but they were seriously putting on the right clothes for the upcoming weather that day. OK, this is web-only now, but hell, what a great idea. Seriously.

PRIMA TV

TV Nova's rival is PRIMA TV, which broadcasts *Show Jana Krause* (an edgier Czech version of *The David Letterman Show*). Many Czech housewives dig *Prostřeno* ("It's set up"), a popular late-afternoon cooking show. But the real backbone of PRIMA TV programming is the crime news—*Krimi zprávy* ("Crime News") and *Krimi Plus* ("Crime Plus")—and celebrity gossip news—*VIP Zprávy* ("VIP News") and *Top Star Magazín* ("Top Star Show"). They've also got your *Bones*, *Desperate Housewives* or *Will & Grace* along with game shows, spin-offs and domestic soaps.

Nova Sport Channel

All your sports, from local to global.

TV BARRANDOV

A relatively new Czech TV channel that broadcasts in digital. There's a plethora of political and lifestyle talk shows, documentaries and sitcoms.

Óčko TV

MTV anyone? Except *Óčko*'s got more viewer interaction—people can vote for songs via text or the Internet. Natural, since you can also watch this cable station online.

FOR THE KIDS)))
PRO DĚTI

The Little Eveninger
Večerníček
In the U.S., kids know the Disney versions of fairytale classics. In the Czech Republic, it's the long-running evening show *Večerníček* providing that memory. The program is named after the main character, a little cartoon boy on a hobbyhorse, who greets visitors with *Dobrý večer!* before the cartoon and then signs off with *Dobrou noc!* at the end of the show. These are the most popular classics from the series:

About a Little Mole
O krtkovi
This short seven-minute animated show features a little mole who completes unusual and funny tasks while traveling the country.

Pat & Mat
A je to!
A puppet animation show chronicles the funny tales of Pat and Mat, two clumsy handymen.

Czech Robin Hood
Rumcajs
Once a good-hearted shoemaker, Rumcajs falls out with the local nobility, becomes a bandit and moves to the woods with his family where he proceeds to steal from the rich to help the poor.

Fairy Tale at Krkonošské Mountain
Krkonošské pohádky
About a mean, rich farmer, Trauntenberg, and his two servants, Anče and Kuba, who are under a patronage of the mountain Lord of Weather named Krakonoš. Krakonoš always sides with the underdogs and manages to punish Trauntenberg.

Grandma never misses watching her variety shows on TV.
Babička si nikdy nenechá ujít sledování **televarieté** *v televizi.*
There are several *Saturday Night Live*–like variety shows where celebrities do funny sketches with bands and circus acts thrown in. Not all at once of course. This is the kind of shit Czechs love.

Turn on the tube, the news is on!
Zapni telku, dávaj zprávy!

Quit channel surfing—I'm getting dizzy!
Přestaň přepínat tu televizi—už se mi z toho motá hlava!

Pass me the remote.
Podej mi ovládání.

Stop staring at the box and let's go out!
Přestaň čumět na bednu a pojď ven!

My favorite show is…
Můj oblíbenej pořad je…

I hate that stupid…
Nesnáším tu blbost…

> **Survivor.**
> *Trosečník.*
>
> **Deal or No Deal.**
> *Ber nebo neber.*
>
> **Dancing with the Stars.**
> *Star dance.*
>
> **Kitchen Nightmares.**
> *Ano šéfe!*
>
> **CSI: Miami.**
> *Kriminálka Miami.*
>
> **Spongebob Squarepants.**
> *Spongebob v kalhotách.*
>
> **Hospital at the End of the City.**
> *Nemocnice na kraji města.*
> This TV series about doctors in a small city hospital is only in reruns now, but it was incredibly popular during its run in the late 1970s and remains an addictive classic for all generations.
>
> **Arabela.**
> *Arabela.*
> An '80s classic with many Czech stars. It's about a family from the real world who interact with a royal family from the Kingdom of Fairy Tales. Funny, poetic and loved by all generations.

·····Radio
Rádio

Czechs listen to the radio a lot, which means a crowded field
for those ears. You'll find news and political talk, domestic
and American pop, British pop/rock and morning talk shows.
But there's also a lot of boring crap on, so choose your radio
station wisely.

Turn it to...
Nalaď tam...

I only listen to...
Já poslouchám jenom...

Rádiožurnál.
National radio station with news and opinion journalism.

Radio Prague.
International news broadcast in six languages, baby!
If you're wondering, they're Czech, English, German,
French, Spanish and Russian.

Vltavu.
Classical, jazz and artsy culture programs.

Rádio 1.
Alternative and independent music (jazz, reggae, ambient,
punk, etc.). Oh, and it's one of the few Czech radio
stations to have some shows hosted by English-speaking
DJs.

Rádio Impuls.
The most popular Czech station; you'll hear a combo of
pop, news, traffic and entertainment.

Evropu 2.
The playlist: top pop songs in Europe. The audience:
teens and the "young at heart."

Frekvence 1.
Lots of Czech music, news and lifestyle shows.

Rock Zone.
Alternative rock, punk, metal, etc.

Beat Rádio.
Classic rock (Metallica, Peter Gabriel, Genesis, Neil Young and the likes).

·····Newspapers and magazines
Noviny a časopisy

There's a vibrant café scene in Prague, so if you want to linger over some java and peruse a periodical, here are some to choose from.

The Prague Post
The only English-written weekly newspaper in the CR; it targets English-speaking expats and foreigners living in the Czech Republic. You can also read it online at praguepost.cz.

Blesk
The Lighting
The country's most popular daily tabloid newspaper.

People's News
Lidové noviny
Former dissidents resurrected this newspaper that was published covertly under communist party rule and overtly after the Velvet Revolution. This conservative-leaning daily features everything from politics and economics to science and culture.

Young Front Today
MF DNES
Once the official communist news outlet for youth, today it takes a more right-wing conservative and commercialized stand on the news—think *USA TODAY*. It's the second most circulated paper in Prague.

Metro
Metro
This free daily newspaper is available in Prague and all the other big Czech cities.

Týden
A whopper (over 100 pages) of a magazine, it comes out every Monday.

Reflex
Popular sociopolitical controversial magazine.

Respekt
This weekly liberal mag focuses on investigative journalism and PC crap like ecofriendliness and multiculturalism.

Čtyřlístek
Four-leaf clover
Published since 1969, this comic book is filled with stories about four friends: a smart cat, a pretty dog, a happy-go-lucky pig and a cheeky rabbit.

Where's the nearest news kiosk?
Kde je tady nejbližší kiosek s novinama?

How much is this comic book?
Kolik stojí tenhle komiks?

Grab me a pack of cigarettes at the newsstand.
Vyzvedni mi u stánku krabičku cigaret.

Trafika
These little shops sell newspapers, magazines, tobacco products, postcards and stamps. You can also buy lottery tickets there and become a millionaire (the most popular tickets are *Sportka* and *Mates*).

·····Movies
Filmy

Czechs *love* films, especially homegrown ironic (or dark) comedies that often outdraw the Hollywood flicks. But don't worry, if you absolutely gotta see that Tinseltown release, big-budget American (and other foreign) movies screen soon after their world premieres and are usually shown in the original language with Czech subtitles.

Let's go to the movies.
Pojď do bijáku.

Do you have *Up and Down* on DVD?
Máš Horem pádem na dývýdýčku?

***The Country Teacher* is the only Czech film I've seen so far.**
Venkovský učitel je jedinej českej film, kterej jsem zatím viděl.

This…flick turned out to be a flop.
Ten/ta/to…je propadák.

This…always puts me in a good mood.
Tenhle/tahle/tohle…mi vždycky zvedne náladu.

WELCOME TO CZECH HOLLYWOOD)))
VÍTEJTE V ČESKÉM HOLLYWOODU

Czech cinematography is well-known around the world thanks to Oscar-winning directors like Miloš Forman (*One Flew Over the Cuckoo's Nest*, *Amadeus*) and Jan Svěrák (*Kolya*). Not to mention the excellent filming locations in Prague and other parts of the country. And when American directors want to get things done here, they call on Barrandov Studios (one of the biggest and most sought after set of film studios in Europe), known as the "European Hollywood" for its exceptional production services and facilities. A bit conceited? Not really—they have the resume to back up that nickname: The Mission Impossible flicks, the Bourne Identity series, *Casino Royale* and *The Chronicles of Narnia: Prince Caspian* have all been filmed on location in the Czech Republic in association with Barrandov Studios.

tearjerker
doják

romance
slaďák

screwball comedy
bláznivá komedie

chick flick
film pro baby

cartoon
animovaný film

Western
kovbojka

suspense
kriminálka

documentary
dokumentární film

B movie
béčkovej film

porn
porno

Dubbed movies are better than **subtitled** ones.
Dabovaný filmy jsou lepší než s titulkama.

The **line** starts back there!
Fronta začíná támhle!

No cuts!
Nepředbíhej!

How many **tix** do we need to buy?
Kolik lupenů potřebujem koupit?

·····The stage
Jeviště

Unlike in the U.S., theater is a big part of Czech culture. So if you imagine it's all about tight-bunned ballerinas and classical music, you'd be wrong. It's modern, it's fast-paced and it's a whole lot hipper than you might think.

Modern dance
Moderní tanec
For those of you who are not into the whole classical ballet thing, you might wanna catch one of the modern dance companies that usually incorporate experimental and multimedia techniques (420 people, TOW, Dot 504 and Nanohách put on some great shows).

Puppet theater
Loutkové divadlo
A folk tradition, Czech puppet theater is a trip. There's something bizarre and magical about watching marionettes singing Don Giovanni operas. Prague's International Institute of Marionette Arts (*Mezinárodní institut loutkářského umění*) has performances that reflect the city's dark and satirical humor. For daily child-friendly shows, head to Divadlo DRAK.

Black-light theater
Černé divadlo
Black-light theater features a darkened stage, black lighting, performers in fluorescent costumes and alternative music

that combine to create a crazy visual illusion. It's sort of like
watching human-sized neon signs move across a pitch-
black stage. There are many black-light theaters throughout
Prague; two of the favorites are *Laterna Magika* and *Jiří Srnec
Black Light Theatre*.

I definitely wanna get high before we see that H.I.L.T.
performance.
Během pobytu v Praze se chci definitivně zkouřit a vidět
představení *H.I.L.T.*

Geared to a young, hip crowd, H.I.L.T. (Hoidekr Interactive
Light Theatre) shows are more alternative with modern music
like techno and electronic. Very cool.

Did you get tickets for a **matinee** at the Theater of
Spejbl and Hurvínek?
*Sehnal jsi lístky na **odpolední představení** do Divadla
Spejbla a Hurvínka?*

Divadlo Spejbla a Hurvínka has been featuring comic stories
with the main puppet Hurvínek (a nosy and adventurous
boy) since 1930s. The short stories are also a big hit on TV
as a part of the *Little Eveninger* (*Večerníček*) series, and the
Hurvínek 3D movie was released a while ago.

I feel like seeing some modern dance tonight.
Dnes bych chtěl / chtěla vidět moderní tanec.

Can you recommend a good puppet show?
Můžeš mi doporučit dobré loutkové představení?

Where can I buy a souvenir marionette for my mom?
Kde můžu koupit loutku jako suvenýr pro mojí mámu?

Do you get off by watching the dancers run across the stage?
Rajcuje tě, když sleduješ tanečníky / tanečnice pobíhat po jevišti?

·····Music
Hudba

Let's face it: You haven't heard Czech pop music outside the country's borders because it's just not that good. Most songs are just crappy covers of American and British hits sung in Czech. (Yes, there are exceptions to the rule—Monkey Business, NightWork, Ewa Farna and Olga Lounová to name a few new rad artists. But come on, who wants to hear "I'll Be Missing You" in Czech? There are a number of decent alternative, folk-rock and punk bands that perform in Czech or English.

Where can we catch a live concert around here?
Kde tady můžeme jít na živej koncert?

This cool band is playing at the O2 Arena.
Tahle skvělá skupina má koncert v O2 Aréně.

I totally dig Charlie Straight's new album.
Totálně žeru nový album od Charlie Straight.

Track number 3 is da bomb!
Píseň číslo tři je pecka!

Crank it up!
Vokuř to!

Chinaski is on tour this summer.
Chinaski má v létě turné.

Zuzana listens only to Hana Zagorová and other pop chanteuses.
Zuzana poslouchá jenom Hanu Zagorovou a jiné popové šansony.

Where can I get a Karel Gott CD?
Kde seženu cédéčko Karla Gotta?
Known as the Czech Elvis or Mistr (the Champion), Karel Gott (literally, "Charles God") is one of the few singers who made it big abroad. He's been around since the late 1960s and is still the shit in the Czech pop music scene.

Lenka's fucking the DJ at Roxy and he'll let us in for free.
Lenka šuká dýdžeje v Roxy a ten nás tam dostane zadara.

Štěpán always wanted to be a…
Štěpán chtěl být vždycky muzikant…

> **musician.**
> *muzikant.*
>
> **lead singer.**
> *frontman.*
>
> **drummer.**
> *bubeník.*
>
> **guitar player.**
> *kytarista.*
>
> **composer.**
> *skladatel.*

I didn't know stage diving was still in.
Nevěděl / Nevěděla jsem, že skákání do kotle je furt in.
As you probably already noticed, most music styles come from the English-speaking countries and the names are the same in Czech just pronounced with a Slavic accent, so the more English you speak, the hipper you'll appear to Czech speakers when discussing the latest news in the top-40 pop charts.

...music rocks!
*...hudba je **skvělá!***

Pop
Pop

Lucie Bílá is the epitome of a Czech pop diva; her style ranges from funk to heavy metal. I know, strange but true.

Folk
Folková

Acoustic
Akustická

Alternative
Alternativní

Electronica
Elektronická

Classical
Vážná

Country
Kántry

And now for the easy part: Rock, jazz, bluegrass, punk, hip-hop, rap, blues, soul, disco, industrial and R&B are the same in Czech and English.

·····Fashion
Móda

Surrounded by the biggest European fashionistas (France, Italy and Britain), Czechs are always influenced and inspired by the newest styles, so try to keep up with them. In some parts of the world it might be cool to dress casual and frumpy in a hoody and flip-flops, but that sure doesn't fly in the Czech Republic. People here embrace the trendy but usually keep it a few notches below Lady Gaga. I mean, a meat dress at a business meeting may be a little too much.

What should I wear tonight?
Co si mám dnes večer vzít na sebe?

I'm tired of my preppy style.
Už mě nebaví můj slušňáckej styl.

Can you wear something trendier?
Můžeš si vzít na sebe něco víc in?

Linda is stylish.
Linda má styl.

You look really sexy in this dress.
V těch šatech vypadáš fakt sexy.

That outfit makes you look like a hooker.
V tomhle vohozu vypadáš jak šlapka.

She looks like a model no matter what she's wearing.
Vypadá jak modelka, ať má na sobě cokoliv.

Your brother's so heavy metal! Tell him to get a haircut.
Tvůj brácha je takovej metalák! Řekni mu, ať se jde ostříhat.

So this is where all the emo kids hang out.
Tak tady se scházej Emáci / Emačky.

He / She dresses like a...
Oblíká se jako...

> **punk.**
> *pankáč / pankačka.*
>
> **rocker.**
> *roker / rokerka.*
>
> **homeless man / woman.**
> *bezdomovec / bezdomovkyně.*
>
> **skater.**
> *skejťák / skejťačka.*

·····Surfing the web
Serfování na webu

Computer nerds in the Czech Republic love the Internet as much as computer nerds all around the world. Social networking sites and blogs attract a lot of traffic, as do the websites offering pirated movies and music. And, of course, porn's right up there.

Laptop
Laptop

Notebook
Noťas

Computer
Počítač

E-mail
Mejl

Attachment
Příloha

Our building has free wi-fi.
Náš barák má wifinu zadarmo.

Are you on your comp again?
Zase sedíš na kompu?

I just need to download some files.
Musím jenom stáhnout nějaké soubory.

Can you burn me that DVD?
Můžeš mi vypálit to dývýdýčko?

What's your user name?
Jaké je tvoje uživatelské jméno?
Czech computer nerds also use the word "nick."

My password is case-sensitive.
Moje heslo je závislé na velikosti písmen.

I accidentally deleted everything in my inbox.
Omylem jsem vymazal všechno v boxu doručené pošty.

Denise IMs all day when she's at work.
Denisa je na chatu celej den, když je v práci.

Adam is such a lamer, he still doesn't know how to…
Adam je láma, pořád ještě neví, jak…
A lamer, by the way, is someone who majorly lacks netiquette.

   save changes.
   uložit změny.

   use a USB drive.
   používat flešku.

   play MP3s.
   spustit empiny.

   upload a game.
   uploadovat hru.

We still haven't met IRL.
Ještě jsme se nepotkali v reálu.

My PC just crashed.
Spadlo mi písíčko.

Do you use a Czech keyboard?
Používáš českou klávesnici?

Can you Google it for me?
Můžeš mi to vygůglovat?

Someone hacked into my Facebook account.
Někdo mi heknul stránky na Facebooku.

I can't log in.
Nemůžu se zalogovat.

Can you forward it to me before signing out?
Můžeš mi to přeposlat, než se odloguješ?

Try to search for it on the net.
Zkus to vyhledat na netu.

·····Chat and text messaging
Chatování a SMSky

Text speak. A melodic mix of Czech, phonetic Slavic and global English. It just rolls off your finger tips.

ENGLISH	CZECH	TEXT
Hi.	*Ahoj.*	Ah
Thank God.	*Bohudíky.*	Bhd
Ciao ciao.	*Čau, čau.*	CC
Miss ya.	*Chybíš mi.*	Chm
I want you.	*Chci tě.*	Chtě
What is it?	*Co to je?*	Ctj?
What?	*Cože?*	Cž?
Thanks.	*Díky.*	Ď
Fuck you!	*Di do prdele!*	DDP!
It's going well.	*Jde to.*	Dt
Face-to-face	*Tváří v tvář*	F2F
Congrats	*Gratulace*	Gz
Bitch	*Kurva*	Kva
Dick	*Kokot*	Kkt
I love you.	*Miluju tě.*	Mljt
Take care.	*Měj se fajn.*	Msf
I like you.	*Mám tě rád.*	Mtr
You're welcome.	*Nemáš zač.*	Nmz
No, no.	*Ne, ne.*	Nn
Bye-bye.	*Pá, pá.*	Pp
Cheers!	*Zdar!*	Zd

CHAPTER 8

SPORTY CZECH
SPORTOUNÍ ČEŠTINA

Whether playing or cheering, sports play a big role in everyday Czech life. You'll really notice the passion during international competitions like the World Cup and the Ice Hockey World Championships (two of the country's most popular sports that the Czechs also often happen to rock at). *Jedém Češi, jedém!* (Go Czechs, go!)

•••••Ice hockey
Lední hokej

The Czechs have been dominating in ice hockey for decades. In the past few years they've snagged Olympic bronze and silver medals, with the coveted gold coming in 2010. The American NHL teams also rely heavily on the Czech Republic's incredible talent. Ever heard of Dominik Hašek (the Dominator), Jaromír Jágr, Tomáš Vokoun or Patrik Eliáš? Yup—they're Czechs. In fact, there are about 60 Czech players in the NHL, making them the third-largest nationality in the league after Canadians and Americans.

Team
Tým ; Mužstvo

Player
Hráč / Hráčka

Forward
Útočník / Útočnice

Center
Centr

Left wing
Levé křídlo

Right wing
Pravé křídlo

Defenseman
Obránce / Obránkyně

Goalie
Brankář / Brankářka

Are all Czechs obsessed with watching Extraliga?
Všichni Češi jsou posedlý sledováním extraligy?
Extraligy is the ČR's equivalent of the NHL.

Did you see how he slammed that puck into the net?
Viděl / Viděla jsi, jak střelil ten puk do branky?

The ref called a fucking power play!
Ten rozhodčí teď odpískal přesilovku!

They got whooped in overtime.
Projeli to v prodloužení.

Sýkora scored two goals in the second third.
Sýkora dal dva góly ve druhé třetině.

Havlát was suspended for cross-checking and high-sticking.
Havláta poslali dvakrát na trestnou lavici za krosček a za hru vysokou holí.

The ČR national anthem is the jam!
Česká národní hymna je nářez!

·····Soccer
Fotbal

Like for ice hockey, Czechs go ape-shit for soccer. During the season, everyone eats, drinks and breathes the sport. The premier pro league to watch is Gambrinus liga. Sounds like a draft you had last night at the pub? Well, you're right—the league is sponsored by Gambrinus, one of the country's most popular beers. If you want to improve your chances of winning a bet, put your money on AC Sparta Praha, SK Slavia Praha or FC Baník Ostrava, the top teams in the league. And who are the Peles of Czech soccer? Pavel Nedvěd, Petr Čech, Milan Baroš and Tomáš Rosický are all superstars.

That...is da bomb shiznit!
Ten...je prostě bomba!

Damn, that…sucks.
Sakra, ten…je na hovno.

> **team**
> *tým ; mužstvo*
>
> **club**
> *klub*
>
> **striker**
> *útočník / útočnice*
>
> **defender**
> *obránce / obránkyně*
>
> **sweeper**
> *libero*
>
> **coach**
> *trenér / trenérka*
>
> **referee**
> *rozhodčí*

How do we get to the stadium?
Jak se dostaneme na stadión?

Go find out how much that scalper wants for the tickets.
Zjisti, kolik chce ten překupník za lístky.

What's the score?
Kolik to je?

Who's…?
Kdo…?

> **playing today**
> *dnes hraje*
>
> **winning**
> *vede*
>
> **losing**
> *prohrává*
>
> **ball**
> *vykopává*

Which soccer player sucks today?
Jakej fotbalista to dnes sere?

What an awesome header!
To byla boží hlavička!

That...
Ten...

> **goalie is totally stiff!**
> *brankář je úplný dřevo!*
> Literally, "wood."

> **ref's pulling out a yellow card!**
> *sudí vytahuje žlutou kartu!*

> **dumb-ass just kicked the ball into his own post!**
> *blbec teď kopl míč do vlastní brány!*

Let's grab a few beers at halftime.
Pojď si dát o poločasu pár piv.

When Czechs aren't watching soccer, they're living it.

I have to pick up my brother from soccer practice.
Musím vyzvednout bráchu z fotbalového tréninku.

Where can I play some soccer around here?
Kde si tady můžu zahrát fotbal?

Right here—pass the ball!
Tady—přihraj!

You may think you're Pavel Nedvěd, but you'll never be like him.
Ty si myslíš, že jsi Pavel Nedvěd, ale nemáš na něj.

•••••Other sports
Další sporty

Tennis
Tenis
Tennis greats Ivan Lendl and Martina Navrátilová have really spurred interest in this sport. You can find courts everywhere because Czechs play tennis all year round.

Do you wanna go to play a tennis tournament next Sunday?
Chceš si příští neděli zahrát tenisový turnaj?

Do you have an extra racquet I can borrow?
Máš extra raketu na půjčení?

Watch this, he's / she's shooting one ace after another.
Dívej na to, střílí jedno eso za druhým.

Do you wanna play doubles?
Chcete si zahrát dabl?

Nice set!
Pěknej set!

Where are the tennis courts around here?
Kde jsou tady v okolí tenisové kurty?

I play…
Já hraju…

Wanna go play…?
Chceš si zahrát…?

> **dodgeball**
> *vybíjenou*
>
> **football tennis**
> *nohejbal*
>
> **indoor soccer (futsal)**
> *sálovou kopanou (futsal)*
>
> **golf**
> *golf*
>
> **basketball**
> *basket*
>
> **handball**
> *házenou*
> Two teams of seven pass the ball back and forth until someone throws it into the opposing team's goal.

floorball.
florbal.
A simplified indoor version of field hockey.

racquetball.
squash.

Let's see if there's any...on TV.
Pojď se podívat, jestli v televizi dávaj...

boxing
box

beach volleyball
plážový volejbal

gymnastics
gymnastiku

swimming
plavání

surfing
serfování

auto racing
Formuli 1

I can't wait to watch...
Nemůžu se dočkat, až uvidím...

the sports news.
sportovní události.

the ski competitions.
závody v lyžování.

the women's field hockey qualifying rounds.
kvalifikace žen v pozemním hokeji.

the ČR kick Russia's asses.
jak Česko nakope Rusákům prdel.

·····The fans
Fanoušci

Czech fans know how to root for their favorite teams—the louder and more passionate the better. Adding to the subtle adoration are the fans' rabid scarf-waving (in club colors, of course), raucous chanting and drunken screaming (encouraging their team and insulting the other). Yeah, it's a rowdy crowd (there are a handful of die-hards who won't be nominated for the Nobel Peace Prize), so don't be too much of an asshole or you might be contending with riot police or even worse, "ultras," overly enthusiastic fanatics, most often seen at soccer games.

Who do you root for?
Komu fandíš?

Your team sucks ass!
Tvůj tým je na hovno!

Did you see that shit scam!?
Viděl jsi tu sviňárnu!?

They should get a penalty shot for that!
Za to měli dostat penaltu!

Goal!
Gól!

Let's go, Czechlands, let's go!
Do toho, Čechy, do totho!

Move it!
Makéj!

Hey we're gonna kick your ass bad today!
Hele, dnes vám pořádně nakopem prdel!

What the hell are you performing over there?
Co to tam kruci předvádíš?

Why are you shitting yourself over there?
Co se tam s tím sereš?
It's just like the Czechs to use a shit term to describe someone as playing sloppy and slow.

Boys, let's put up a fight!
Kluci, bojujem!

Fuck yeah, we tore them up!
Kurva jó, rozcupovali jsme je na kusy!

·····The Olympic Games
Olympijské hry

There are other countries besides the U.S., Russia and Germany that medal in the Olympics. In fact, Czechs rule in canoeing, shooting and in most things on ice or snow. So in your face!

Do you think we'll get the silver in downhill skiing?
Myslíš, že získáme stříbro ve sjezdu?

Last time we snatched two golds and four bronze.
Minule jsme urvali dvě zlaté a čtyři bronzové.

Where are the next Winter Olympics?
Kde se koná příští Zimní Olympiáda?

Martina Sáblíková won three medals for speed skating.
Martina Sáblíková vyhrála tři medaile v rychlobruslení.

Did you watch the men's aerials last night?
Sledoval / Sledovala jsi včera akrobatické skoky mužů?

I'm a sucker for women's figure skating.
Ženské krasobruslení fakt žeru.

Dude, snowboarding is where it's at.
Frajere, snowbordování je teď in.

In the winter season, I wanna practice...
V zimní sezóně chci trénovat...

> **slalom racing.**
> *slalom.*

> **alpine combined.**
> *alpskou kombinaci.*

> **cross-country skiing.**
> *běh na lyžích.*

> **sledding.**
> *sáňkování.*

> **bobsledding.**
> *bobování.*

I always watch the Summer Olympics.
Vždycky sleduju letní Olympiádu.

Nice shotput!
Pěknej vrh koulí!

Did you see that guy sprinting? He's fuckin' quick!
Viděl jsi toho kluka sprintovat? Je rychlej jak blázen!

My canoe is bigger than yours.
Vidíš, moje kánoj je větší než ta tvoje.

That javelin throw was flawless.
Ten hod oštěpem neměl chybu.

My favorite summer sport is...
Můj oblíbený letní sport je...

> **track and field.**
> *lehká atletika.*

> **hurdling.**
> *běh přes překážky.*

> **diving.**
> *potápění.*

> **trampolining.**
> *skoky na trampolíně.*

·····Exercise
Cvičení

Even though Czech peeps like to stay fit and active, it seems like they don't get too worked up about it. There's definitely a gym scene, but it's more about socializing, meeting new people and burning a few calories before hitting the pub.

Let's hit the gym.
Pojď do posilovny.

This fitness center is rad!
Tohle fitko je parádní!

How do you stay in such good shape?
Jak se udržuješ v takhle dobrý kondici?

I do...every day.
Dělám / Chodím na...každý den.

> **yoga**
> *yógu*
>
> **stretching**
> *strečink*
>
> **breathing exercises**
> *dechová cvičení*
>
> **kickboxing**
> *kickbox*
>
> **bodybuilding**
> *kulturistiku*
>
> **spinning**
> *spinning*
>
> **aerobics**
> *aerobik*
>
> **martial arts**
> *bojová umění*
>
> **jujitsu**
> *jiu jitsu*
>
> **judo**
> *džudo*

meditation
meditaci

Jára does...three times a week.
Jára dělá...třikrát týdně.

push-ups
kliky

sit-ups
sedy-lehy

squats
dřepy

pull-ups
shyby

Today I worked on my core and back.
Dnes jsem jel / jela břišní svaly a záda.

My...is / are so sore.
Pěkně mě bolí...

muscles
svaly

triceps
tricepsy

pecs
prsní svaly

thighs
stehna

glutes
hýždě

Is there a / an...in here?
Je tady někde...?

treadmill
trenažér

stair machine
stepper

exercise bike
rotoped

pool
bazén

sauna
sauna

drinking fountain
pítko s vodou

snack bar
občerstvení

men's / women's locker room
pánská / dámská šatna

quiet room
odpočinková místnost

He's been lifting weights recently, he's **yoked**.
*Poslední dobou posiluje s činkama, je **vymakanej**.*

Tellin' ya, the dude is a **diesel**.
*Ti řikám, ten borec je **vazba**.*

That was a tough **workout**!
*Tohle **posilování** mi dalo zabrat!*

Bára **jumps rope** like a maniac.
*Bára **skáče přes švihadlo** jak maniak.*

Four rounds of **sprints** totally knocked me out.
*Čtyři kola **sprintu** mě totálně vyřídili.*

This **group exercise class** always kicks my ass.
*Tohle **skupinové cvičení** mi dá vždycky zabrat.*

Eww…you're **sweating** like a pig.
*Fujtajbl…**potíš** se jako prase.*

My whole body's sore.
Bolí mě celý tělo.
You can also say *Bolí mě celej člověk*, or literally, "My whole human sores."

·····The great outdoors
Rekreace v přírodě

Czechs are super outdoorsy. Not only do they like to walk everywhere no matter how friggin' cold it is, but they spend a lot of time in the open air enjoying sweet, sweet nature. Many people have countryside cabins or cottages where they spend weekends and holidays, sometimes even winter or summer vacations depending on the location. So in the dead cold of winter it's all about snowboarding, ice skating, sledding and cross-country skiing. And when it's warm, Czechs are into hiking, camping, gardening and picking fruit or collecting mushrooms.

Wanna go…?
Chceš jít…?

jogging
běhat

biking
jezdit na kole

hiking
na výlet

camping
stanovat ; kempovat

rock climbing
lézt po skalách

skydiving
skákat s padákem

hang out by the pool
k bazénu

ice skating
bruslit

sledding
sáňkovat

fishing
chytat ryby

mushroom hunting
na houby

strawberry picking
sbírat jahody

We'll be **sunbathing** all weekend at our cottage by the Lipno dam.
Celý víkend se budeme opalovat na chatě u Lipna.

Let's make a **campfire**, grill some wursts and play guitar.
Pojďme si dnes udělat táborák, opékat buřty a hrát na kytaru.

Novák's family spends every summer on the old **houseboat** in Slapy.
Novákovi tráví každé léto na starém housbótu na Slapech.

·····Games

Hry

Darts
Šipky

Bowling
Kuželky

Pool
Kulečník

Cards
Karty

Dominoes
Domino

Chess
Šachy

Let's play Concentration.
Pojď si zahrát Pexeso.
You know this game by many names (Concentration, Memory, Pairs). Cards are placed face down and you flip two at a time. If they don't match, you flip them back over and try again on your next turn.

David wants to play Ludo all the time.
David chce pořád hrát "Člověče, nezlob se!"
Ludo is just like American Parcheesi—it's a bastardization of the Indian game called Pachisi.

Eva and Mirek are playing **badminton** in the backyard.
*Eva a Mirek hrajou na zahradě **badminton**.*

Hey lazy, how 'bout a game of **Ping-Pong**?
*Ty lenochu, co si takhle zahrát **ping-pong**?*

CHAPTER 9

HUNGRY CZECH
HLADOVÁ ČEŠTINA

Hungry Czechs don't mess around. Hefty portions of hearty, home-cooked grub are washed down with a big mug of lager or a half-liter of Moravian. So get ready for mountains of meat, dumplings and potatoes prepared a hundred different ways. As the Czech proverb says *Hlad je nejlepší kuchař* ("Hunger is the best cook").

•••••Hunger
Hlad

I'm...
Mám...

hungry.
hlad.

starving.
hlad jak vlk.
Literally, "hungry as a wolf."

fucking hungry.
hlad jako prase.
Literally, "I'm hungry as a pig."

I'm dying of hunger.
Umírám hlady.

Her eyes are cross-eyed she's so hungry.
Get her a burger.
Už šilhá hlady. Dej jí hamburger.

My stomach is grumbling.
Kručí mi v břiše.

I can't think on an empty stomach.
S prázdným žaludkem mi to nemyslí.

I gotta eat something.
Musím si dát něco k jídlu.

I have the munchies.
Mám na něco chuť.
You don't have to smoke a bowl to *mít na něco chuť*, you just crave something tasty.

When I get home, I'm gonna pig out.
Až přijdu domů, tak se nažeru.

Dude, let's stuff our faces!
Frajere, pojď si nacpat panděra!
Literally, "stuff our guts."

Radim gorged himself on wursts again.
Radim se zas přecpal párkama.

I'm fucking stuffed.
Nacpal / Nacpala jsem se jako prase.
Literally, "stuffed as a pig."

I'm so full, my stomach is gonna burst.
Jsem tak plnej / plná, že mi praskne břicho.

I overdid it.
Přehnal / Přehnala jsem to.

I'm not gonna be able to eat all that.
Tohle nikdy nemůžu sníst.

Your eyes were bigger than your stomach.
Měl / Měla si velký voči.

·····Food

Jídlo

Salad-eating, nonfat-latte-drinking types beware—traditional Czech grub ain't your thang. So unbutton your pants and dig into some great-tasting garlicky roast meat (pork, beef, duck, goose, rabbit or wild game) usually smothered in butter, lard and a thick warm sauce (dill and cream, paprika, tomato, and mushroom are some favorites).

> **What do you like to eat?**
> *Co rád / ráda jíš?*
>
> **What're your favorite dishes?**
> *Jaký jídla máš rád / ráda?*
>
> **Wanna grab…?**
> *Chceš si dát…?*

some **grub**
nějakej dlabanec

a **bite**
něco k zakousnutí

something **tasty**
nějakou baštu

something **filling**
něco vydatnýho

Bon appetit!
Dobrou chuť!
Unless you're a rude pig, you should give a *Dobrou chuť* to anyone you're dining with.

Put the food on the table!
Nos na stůl!

Let's chow down!
Pojďme se nadlábnout!

C'mon, **help yourself**.
No tak, dej si.

Marek is an **eating machine**.
Marek je žrout.

He never says no to **free eats**.
Nikdy neodmítne, když má šanci se nadlábnout zadarmo.

Our hotel has a breakfast **buffet**.
Náš hotel má snídani formou švédských stolů.
Literally, "Swedish table," or smorgasbord.

I always crave something **greasy** and **fatty** when I'm hungover.
Když mám kocovinu, mám vždycky chuť na něco mastného a tučného.

I'm not a fan of **spicy** sauces.
Nejsem fanda/fanynka ostrých omáček.

Míla's got a major sweet tooth.
Míla je na sladké.

I'm a vegetarian.
Jsem vegetarián / vegetariánka.
While traditional Czech food is meaty, you can find vegetarian-friendly stuff at any restaurant.

Do you know where there's a health food store around here?
Víš kde je tu obchod se zdravou výživou?

Vlasta only eats organic.
Vlasta jí jenom bio potraviny.

I want my food without preservatives please.
Chtěl / chtěla bych jídlo uvařené bez konzervačních látek, prosím.
If you ask for your food without *preservativ*, your server may laugh in your face. (*Preservativ* means "condom" in Czech.)

We cook with GMO-free products only.
Vaříme pouze z produktů bez GMO.

Fuck me, garlic again?!
To mě poser, zase česnek?!

Don't worry about going hungry while you're traveling—Czechs are always welcoming people into their homes for some good ol' Grandma's cooking. Here are some useful phrases if you're lucky enough to get an invite to a private house.

Mom's home-cooked dinners are the best.
Doma uvařená večeře od mámy chutná nejlíp.

My compliments to the cook.
Posílám kompliment kuchařovi.

Can I get a second helping?
Můžu si přidat?

I had more than enough.
Měl / Měla jsem víc než dost.

That smells excellent!
To voní výborně!

·····Restaurants and pubs
Restaurace a hospody

Czechs bring a competitive edge to anything they do, including visits to the pub. Competitions center around your ability to consume massive amounts of beer and shots along with sausages, dumplings or whatever can be stuffed into your mouth. And if even after such debauchery you can still be coherently witty when commenting on politics, sex or current events, you've reached the finals of the pub Olympics.

Let's go out to eat!
Pojď se někam najíst!

What are you having?
Co si dáš?

What beerhouse serves the best headcheese around here?
Jaká pivnice v okolí má nejlepší tlačenku?

Bring me a…
Přineste mi…

> **menu.**
> *jídelníček.*
>
> **nonalcoholic bev.**
> *nealko.*
>
> **Coke.**
> *kolu.*
>
> **napkin.**
> *ubrousek.*
>
> **fruit soda.**
> *limonádu.*

PUB RULES)))
PRAVIDLA V HOSPODĚ

While pubs promote a casual atmosphere, there are a few guidelines you should follow while getting your pub grub on in the Czech Republic.

WALK IN BEFORE YOUR LADY FRIEND.

Unless you want to risk some douche hitting on your date before you've made your move, enter the pub before the lady.

SEAT YOURSELF.

There sure ain't no cute hostess waiting at the front to take you to your seat. Just find a table and claim your spot. They'll notice you when you walk in.

PREPARE FOR A GROUP DATE.

The pub is a group affair, so if you've come with your date, be open to sitting with a bunch of burly men, 'cause you might have some trouble finding a table for two.

DON'T BE AN ASSHOLE TO THE STAFF.

Just because there's cash burning a hole in your pocket doesn't mean you call the shots. Most servers think the pub can't function without them and that they own the place. So kiss their asses a little (or a lot) and let them come to you. If you wildly wave your hand at them to get their attention, you'll be waiting a long time for those half-liters (*půllitry*) and *přílohy* (sides).

BE PREPARED TO DRINK. DRINK A LOT.

In some of the cheaper pubs, they just keep bringing drinks even if you don't request another round. I mean, that's what you're there for, right?

CLOSE THE TAB FIRMLY.

Put your "I'm not fucking around this time" mug on and repeat the magic words *Já platím* ("I'm paying") or *Účet, prosím* ("Check, please"). Otherwise you're gonna be drinking until the next day.

LEAVE YOUR CREDIT CARDS AT HOME.

Oh, please, if you pull out some plastic in the small local pubs, they'll laugh in your face.

I'd like some...please.
Chtěl / Chtěla bych...prosím.

> **mineral water with no ice**
> *minerálku bez ledu*
>
> **soda water**
> *sodovku*
>
> **juice**
> *džus*
>
> **silverware**
> *příbor*
>
> **bread**
> *chleba*
>
> **ketchup**
> *kečup*
>
> **tartar sauce**
> *tatarku*

Can you pass me the salt and pepper?
Můžeš mi podat sůl a pepř?

Can you get me the check?
Můžete mi donést účet?

Can we order?
Můžeme si objednat?

What's fresh today?
Co máte dneska čerstvého?

What are the...today?
Jaké máte dnes ...?

> *hotovky*
> A ready-to-serve main meal. Because many Czech dishes take forever to cook, pubs and restaurants start preparing some of the dishes in the morning so they're ready to serve for a quick lunch or dinner.
>
> *minutka*
> A dish made when you order it, like steak and fries or chicken breast baked with peaches and Edam cheese.

Shoot, it's taking a long time—did you guys have to go out and catch the trout I ordered?
Doprčic, to je doba. Vy jste toho pstruha, co jsem si oblednal, museli jít teprve ulovit?

Does it come with potatoes or rice?
Je to s bramborama nebo rýží?

I'll have one more portion of dumplings.
Dám si ještě jednu porci knedlíků.

I'll have a steak with mixed greens.
Dám si biftek se zeleninovým salátem.
If you like your meat still beating, ask for it *krvavý* (rare). If it really needs to be dead, you'll want it *dobře propečený* (well-done).

There's a dead fly in my tripe soup, where is the…?
Mám v té dršťkové mouchu, kde je…?

> **owner**
> *majitel / majitelka*
>
> **manager**
> *vedoucí*
>
> **chef**
> *šéfkuchař / šéfkuchařka*
>
> **waiter / waitress**
> *číšník / servírka*

What kind of wine does the sommelier recommend?
Jaké víno doporučuje someliér?

I'm tight on cash, but I could do the dishes to pay for my pork roast.
Mám málo peněz, ale můžu umejt nádobí, abych za tu vepřovou pečeni zaplatil / zaplatila.

•••••Yum!
Mňam!

Tasty!
Dobrota!

It's yummy!
To je bašta!

The cook is a genius.
Ten kuchař je génius.

Wow, you really wolfed it down!
Ty jo, tys to fakt zdlábnul / zdlábla!

This is a real gourmet dish.
To je opravdová delikatesa.

Who wants seconds?
Kdo chce nášup?

He liked his dinner so much that he licked the plate clean.
Olizoval se až za ušima, jak mu ta večeře chutnala.
Literally, "He was licking his ears with his tongue."

Czechs are so stoked about their food that they often use diminutives to talk about it. You'd think you could only use expressions like "have some little soupy" when baby talking to a little kid, but in the Czech Republic it totally flies if you text your tough, macho friend and ask him, *Hele, zajdem večer na bifteček?* ("Hey, wanna grab some steaky tonight?").

When I come home, my wifey will make some duckling with nice little dumplings and cabbage!
Až přijdu domů, ženuška udělá kachničku s knedlíčkama a se zelím!

I'll have a little piece of that incredible cakey.
Dám si malej kousek toho úžasného dortíčku.

•••••Yuck!
Fuj!

That's disgusting!
To je nechutný!

This raw pork knee looks gross.
Tohle syrový vepřový koleno vypadá hnusně.

This slop is inedible.
Tohle žrádlo se nedá jíst.

Our lunch was totally rank.
Ten náš oběd byl totálně jetej.

Those mashed potatoes look like a pile of shit.
Tyhle šťouchaný brambory vypadaj jako sračka.

That goulash isn't sitting right.
Ten guláš mi nesednul.

I think that fruit is spoiled.
Myslím, že to ovoce je zkažený.

Throw it away, it's rotten.
Vyhoď to, je to shnilý.

I'm not eating that glop.
Tuhle šlichtu nejím.

·····Typical Czech Cuisine
Typická česká kuchyně

Here are some *předkrmy* (appetizers) to warm up your digestive system for the main course…

Ďábelské tousty
Literally, "devil's toasts," these tasty bites are sliced baguettes slathered with spiced ground meat, topped with a cheesy mixture and then baked to gooey perfection.

Plněná vejce
We all know how good deviled eggs are.

Obložená mísa
This is the Czech charcuterie plate of cheeses, preserved meats and pickles.

Šunkové rolky s křenem
Ham rolls filled with horseradish cream.

Olomoucké tvarůžky

Can you say stinky cheese? The semisoft yellow *Olomouc* cheese has a ridiculously pungent taste. It really reeks, but when it's served with fresh bread, butter and a cold beer, it tastes like heaven. It's about as traditional as you get with cheese—Emperor Rudolf II was known to eat it way back in the 16th century.

Tlačenka

This Czech headcheese is sliced, doused with vinegar and served with chopped raw onions. Meaty, offally deliciousness.

Jitrnice

Liverwurst. You'll find it served cold with fresh chopped onions and vinegar. But it can also be roasted or steamed.

Bramboráky

Pan-fried grated potato pancakes—you know, latkes. They can be served as an appetizer or a side dish.

Soups (*polívka*) are popular first-course dishes. There are a lot to choose from and, damn, they're tasty!

Kuřecí s nudličkama

Chicken noodle.

Hovězí vývar s játrovýma knedlíčkama

Beef broth with liver dumplings.

Gulášovka

Goulash soup. Yes. It's a "liquid goulash" with pieces of potatoes and chunks of beef. Yummers!

Zelňačka

Basically sauerkraut soup (cabbage, sour cream and sometimes smoked ham or pork).

Koprovka

Dill soup made with sour milk.

Kulajda

Mushroom soup with potatoes, sour cream and the ever-popular fresh dill.

Česnečka

Warm and cozy, this garlic soup is the perfect hangover cure.

Ready for the meat onslaught? Here are some of the rib-sticking main dishes (*hlavní jídla*).

Vepřová pečeně ; Vepřo knedlo zelo

Pork roast mostly accompanied by dumplings and sauerkraut. This meal is affectionately called by all Czechs *vepřo knedlo zelo*—basically shortened forms of the Czech words for pork (*vepřová*), dumplings (*knedlíky*) and cabbage (*zelí*) or sauerkraut.

Svíčková

Roast beef sirloin covered with a delicious spiced cream sauce infused with root veggies and served, of course, with dumplings.

Řízek

You're probably more familiar with *řízek* by the German term *schnitzel*. The Czech version is usually pork, chicken or veal that's breaded, pan-fried, and served with potato salad or mashed potatoes. Yeah, it's the same thing. You do see carp schnitzel, and it's traditionally served on Christmas Eve.

Guláš

Goulash. You know, meaty (beef of pork) brownish-red paprika stew served with dumplings, potatoes or bread.

Pečené vepřové koleno

Flintstones-sized roasted pork knuckles. Horseradish and mustard are the usual condiments.

Pečená husa

Roasted goose served with dumplings and red cabbage. Another Christmas (and other special occasions) favorite.

And if all that roast meat doesn't fill you up, there's plenty of starchy options from the ubiquitous *knedlíky* (flour or potato dumplings) and *pečené brambory* (roasted potatoes) to *hranolky* (fries) and *rýže* (rice).

·····Sweets
Sladkosti

Koláče
Round, soft pastries topped with fresh fruits, plum paste, jam or poppy seeds and curd. They kinda look like mini pizzas.

Buchty
Any of the above-mentioned *koláče* toppings are tucked into a yeasty dough and formed into little buns. They're then crammed next to each other on a pan and baked. The result is a square of sweet deliciousness.

Buchtičky se šodó
Small sweet buns covered with warm, foamy vanilla or wine cream sauce (*šodó*).

Ovocné knedlíky
Round steaming-hot fruit dumplings covered in melted butter, sugar and curd.

Palačinky
Czech crepes that are served warm and rolled up with fresh fruit, jam or nougat, and a hefty dollop of whipped cream.

Zmrzlinový pohár
You say *zmrzlinový pohár*, I say "ice cream sundae." You can get everything from your traditional hot fudge sundae to a fruit sorbet topped with some fresh fruit, cherry and even egg liquor (*vaječný likér*).

·····The deli
Lahůdky

When they need a quick hunger fix, Czechs head to the *lahůdky* (also called *delikatesy*). You can eat in or take your grub to go. Delis sell a lot of cold or warm meats, salamis, cheeses and a variety of popular *chlebíčky* (small open-faced sandwiches).

Salát

Just like in the U.S., salads can be healthy (mixed greens, *zeleninové saláty*) or caloric bombs (a bunch of things chopped up and smothered in mayo). The most popular mayo salads are:

Vlašský salát

Wallachian salad—potato salad with ham, salami, celery root and green peas.

Hermelínový salát

Hermelín, a Camembert-style Czech cheese, mixed with paprika, bell peppers and raw onion.

Vajíčkový salát

Egg salad.

Bramborový salát

Potato salad.

Chlebíčky

Chlebíčky, "little breads," are tiny open-faced cold sandwiches topped with salad and some salami, ham, salmon or cheese. They usually come with some egg, relish or parsley on top and are a popular quickie lunch choice since they're very tasty and found in a fridge display, premade and ready to scarf.

Many people also bring *chlebíčky* as a hostess gift when visiting a friend's house. In fact, if you're ever invited to a Czech's house in the afternoon, you'll most likely see *chlebíčky* along with cheese, salami and wine, beer or tea. Seems like a lot of food? Well, Czechs always offer you food and drinks. You'll never hear, "Do you want a glass of water?" It's more like, "Do you want food, beer, a shot?"

Utopenci

Literally, "the drowned ones," these are sliced, pickled wursts marinated in vinegar with raw onions, bay leaf and cayenne pepper.

Zavináče

Slices of herring or other white fish are rolled with diced root veggies and cabbage (hence the literal name "the rolled